Convince Them *in* 90 Seconds*

*or less

Make Instant Connections That Pay Off in Business and in Life

by **Nicholas Boothman**

MANJUL

Manjul Publishing House

First published in India by

MANJUL

Manjul Publishing House

• C-16, Sector 3, Noida, Uttar Pradesh 201301, India
Website: www.manjulindia.com
Registered Office:
•2nd Floor, Usha Preet Complex, 42 Malviya Nagar, Bhopal 462 003 - India
Distribution Centres
Ahmedabad, Bengaluru, Kochi, Kolkata, Chennai,
Hyderabad, Mumbai, New Delhi, Pune

First published in the United States as
CONVINCE THEM IN 90 SECONDS OR LESS

Published by arrangement with
Workman Publishing Company, Inc., New York.

This edition first published in India in 2015
Third impression 2025

ISBN 978-81-8322-563-2

Printed and bound in India by Repro India Ltd.

Dedication

For Gracie

Acknowledgments

I want to thank Francis Xavier Muldoon for planting the seeds of this book in my head and my heart, Mike Freedman for showering them with his wisdom, Peter Workman for shedding light upon them, and Margot Herrera, my editor at Workman, for nursing them to full bloom.

Very special thanks to Derek Sweeney of the Sweeney Agency Speaker Bureau for his ceaseless support, advice, and friendship. My deep gratitude to Brian Palmer, Don Jenkins, Susan Masters, and the team at National Speakers Bureau in the U.S. for their ongoing cheerleading.

My heartfelt thanks to Mary and Lester Stanford for welcoming me to these fair shores more than three decades ago and pointing me in all the right directions.

Contents

Introduction: Those Crucial 90 Seconds

This book is not about a new business theory; it's about how you can become more successful in business and life by learning to connect with your customers, clients, colleagues, bosses, employees, and even total strangers in ninety seconds or less.

That first ninety seconds of any encounter isn't just a time for making a good first impression. In the first few moments of any meeting, you connect with a person's instincts and their human nature—their hardwired responses. In the opening seconds, our subconscious survival instincts kick in and our mind and body decide whether to run or fight or interact, whether this person offers an opportunity or a threat, whether they're friend or foe. This book teaches you about the snap judgments that are made in those first few instants and how you can make them work to your advantage. Once you're past those first hurdles and trust is established, you can begin connecting on a person-to-person, or (to be more precise) personality-to-personality, level. I'll show you how to figure out just who and what you're dealing with and how to connect with, as well as motivate, influence, and convince them.

There's an order and a process to connecting with others: First you establish trust with the basic instincts, then you establish rapport with the personality. What results is a relationship, and every relationship holds almost infinite possibilities. How do I know this? From experience. Where I am today is light-years from where I started and where I expected to be when I began my life journey. And I owe much of my success to my ability to connect with people.

I spent a quarter of a century making people look good. I was an international fashion and advertising photographer, and that taught me a lot about making people look appealing. I'm not talking just about shooting professional models. Businesspeople, musicians, jet pilots, and farmers all went before my lens, and I got each of them not only to put their best face forward but to feel as if they'd been confident and charismatic all their life.

Anyone you put in front of a camera has a face, a body, and an attitude—with a message to deliver. My job was to give form to that message by influencing my subjects with my face, body, attitude, voice, and words. In this book you'll learn how to use all these tools—face, body, attitude, voice, along with words and language patterns—to create an impression and get *your* message across in ninety seconds or less.

I'm not going to be taking a photo of you, but I am going to change the image you have of yourself and show you how to connect with anyone and everyone in your daily life—quickly, simply, easily. No matter your line of work, you are first and foremost in the business of connecting with other people—and those people are deciding whether that's going to happen or not, in about the same time it takes to glance at a photograph.

Early on in my photography career, as I circulated among studios and clients in London, Lisbon, Madrid, New York, Cape Town, and Toronto, I became aware that there were certain people who could get along with anyone the moment they met them. And because of this ability, they were able to strike up instant relationships, boost their business reach, and rapidly make their way up the ladder of success. But for everyone I met who could make these fast connections, there were half a dozen who couldn't. It was as if some people were always open for business, while others were closed—at least that's the impression I got when I first met them. But as I got to know these "closed" people better, I saw that first impressions can be deceiving. Most of those who seemed so remote weren't actually like that at all.

Clients, CEOs, models, hair and makeup artists, advertising executives, accountants, decision makers, jet pilots, farmers, musicians—people who more often than not had never met before—would come together at a shoot. Those who were open and able to connect easily and quickly with others flourished, while those who were closed and kept to themselves seemed to miss out on opportunities and lucky breaks and to get left behind. To my surprise, brains, beauty, and talent didn't seem to have anything to do with it.

Certain people seem to have an innate ability to connect with others in a warm, spontaneous way.

Observing, influencing, and portraying behavior and mood make up a large part of a fashion photographer's tool kit, and after a time, I began to recognize patterns of behavior that enabled people to get along—or not get along—with others. Some people play out patterns that work, while others are stuck in patterns that don't.

It was about this time that I became aware of the work being done by Drs. Richard Bandler and John Grinder. They had developed a technique for studying and understanding the structure behind human behavior and how we use language to program ourselves and others. It went by the unwieldy name of Neuro-Linguistic Programming, or NLP for short. NLP lets you see what's behind how we act and allows you to understand how what we say makes us and those around us behave. I soon found myself studying alongside Dr. Bandler in London and New York and earning my credentials in NLP.

Afterward it became increasingly easy for me to observe the patterns of behavior of the people I was encountering every day and figure out specifically how those with good people skills differed in their approach from those without these skills. As I became more successful, I was often invited to lecture on fashion and advertising photography at colleges and clubs. It wasn't long, though, before my talk consisted of five minutes about photography and fifty-five minutes on how to connect with the person on the other side of the lens and get their cooperation. Soon I was invited to give this same talk—minus the five minutes about photography—to airline personnel, at colleges, in hospitals, and to associations. This quickly blossomed into engagements with major corporations all over the world.

As I became more involved with the business world, meeting and connecting with thousands of people, I became aware that connecting in business is different from connecting in your personal life. In your personal life you get to choose your friends, but at work you can't walk away from relationships with your colleagues, employees, superiors, and clients without walking away from your job—you have to build and maintain those relationships every day. This book will show you everything you need to know about connecting with the people you *have to connect with.*

You can choose your friends but you can't choose your coworkers.

Some experts estimate that 15 percent of your financial success is determined by skills and knowledge, while 85 percent comes from your ability to connect with other people and engender trust and respect. Today, whether you're interviewing for a job, making a sale, mentoring a student, or talking with your boss about a raise, the better you are at connecting with other people, the better your chances of success will be. And you have to do it *fast!* People make that "like"/"don't like," "okay"/"no way" decision in ninety seconds or less. How to best handle those ninety seconds is what you'll learn about here.

We're going to cover everything from your nonverbal impact to your personal packaging, from your one-on-one conversation skills to your ability to connect with and influence groups. You'll read about real-life situations that show rather than tell you how to turn new and existing connections to your advantage, as well as a host of techniques and tactics that will help you make the connections you need to thrive in today's hypercompetitive workplace.

One of the pleasures of being a fashion photographer was making people look better than they ever imagined they could. It's exciting to realize that you can look, sound, and feel more significant, more purposeful, and more stunning than you dared to dream—while all the time, underneath, you are still being faithful to your true nature. This book is not about being phony or acting like someone you are not; it's about creating a favorable link between your internal nature with its beliefs and values, and the external world where you go to work.

This book is like one of my fashion photos. It's going to change forever how you see yourself. *Convince Them in 90 Seconds or Less* will give you a significant competitive edge by showing you how to take full advantage of your body, your mind, your voice, and above all, your imagination, to maximize the potential in every relationship, be it business-related, personal, or social.

Part One

The Basics

As a species, we are instinctively driven to come together and win people over to survive, evolve, and do business. Connecting and convincing are elemental forces of human nature that allow this to happen.

The ability to connect and convey your ideas convincingly can be wrapped around a few basic insights so simple that you can get a handle on them while riding around in the back of a taxicab in the rain.

1

Muldoon's Rules: There's No Failure, Only Feedback

My first job was as Francis Xavier Muldoon's personal assistant. Muldoon was advertising manager for *Woman,* the largest-circulation weekly magazine in the U.K. It was the mid-sixties, in England, and my new boss had risen from nowhere to the top of an incredibly competitive business in just three years. Francis Xavier Muldoon was what you might call socially gifted.

What made Muldoon's gift work was "The Gospel According to Muldoon."

"The Gospel According to Muldoon" began with the following: "First impressions set the tone for success more often than class, credentials, education, or what you paid for lunch." In fact, we usually decide within the first two seconds of meeting someone new just how we'll respond to him or her. But don't feel too smug about that—in the same instant, that person is deciding how to respond to you. (By the way, if you're wondering about the other eighty-eight seconds, they are used to confirm and cement the relationship and set up the way you'll communicate from this point on.)

Muldoon's observations were always alarmingly simple: "When people like you, they see the best in you. When they don't, they tend to see the worst. It's common sense, really. If a client likes you, she'll probably interpret your leaping about as enthusiasm, but if she doesn't like you, she'll probably think your jumping around proves you're an idiot."

He was right. An interviewer who likes you might interpret your gentle nature as considerate, while one who doesn't like you might label you as weak. A manager who likes you will find your self-confidence gutsy; one who doesn't will consider you arrogant. One person's genius is another person's jackass. It all depends on how you are reflected in the other person's imagination. "Capture the imagination and you capture the heart," was also part of the Muldoon Gospel, "because life, any way you look at it, right from day one, is about behavior. Imagination triggers emotion, emotion triggers attitude, and attitude drives behavior."

I'd never met anyone like Francis Xavier Muldoon. I'd moved to London from the north of England because

I wanted to be in the middle of exciting things—even though I never really stopped to think what that meant until I got there. I soon realized I was turned on by people who were making things happen. One problem with Muldoon, though, was that for the longest time, I didn't know whether he was a genius or a lunatic.

Muldoon was a genius, but it took a while to figure out what made him so effective. In fact, some of what I had to do for him didn't seem to make any sense at all—at first. My first truly mad assignment for F. X. was to lick, stick, and scribble on the front of 2,467 assorted envelopes and stuff them into an enormous cloth sack. The next afternoon I accompanied the maestro on a sales call to the office of the managing director of a mail-order supply company on Oxford Street. Muldoon looked marvelous—dapper, confident, and happy—and I, with my sack, looked like a grave robber on my way back from collecting a body.

We were shown into the director's office. Francis Xavier Muldoon greeted the prospective client as if they were old friends—almost brothers. He introduced me as his assistant and our host signaled us to sit.

We took our chairs in front of his oversized antique banker's desk. Almost immediately, Francis Xavier smiled and spoke. "With your permission, I have something for you."

"Please, go ahead," said the director, nodding a vague approval.

"Nick here will show you," said Muldoon. That was my cue. Without missing a beat, and armed with a dutiful grimace, I spread a large green canvas sheet on the floor and dumped the entire contents of the sack in the center of it. There were so many envelopes they tumbled onto the floor and against the chairs.

As the dumbfounded man sat there staring at the enormous heap of correspondence, Muldoon, in his gentle yet precise voice, proclaimed, "This is the kind of response you can expect when you advertise with *Woman* magazine." He paused long enough to get the man's attention; then, looking him directly in the eye, Muldoon said, "Two thousand four hundred and sixty-seven responses landed on the desk of one of your competitors in just one day as a direct result of advertising with us. We can do the same for you."

Time expired so far? About ninety seconds.

In the cab on the way back to the office, with a twenty-six-week advertising contract in his briefcase and all 2,467 envelopes stuffed safely back in their sack, Muldoon decided it was time for me to learn a little more about "The Gospel According to Muldoon."

"So what do you think happened back there?" he asked.

"You'd never met the man before?" I asked.

"I hadn't."

"But you were like old friends."

"It certainly felt that way, didn't it?" Muldoon smiled and turned toward me. "Do you have any idea why?"

"He's probably heard of you."

"Can't count on that. I'll tell you what, you sit over there in the jump seat facing me and I'll explain what was going on."

A London taxicab looks a lot like a big, black tin cracker box on wheels, but it is roomy and well suited to the comfortable conveyance of people and luggage. In the back there is a bench seat facing forward and two spring-loaded jump seats facing backward. I pushed down the jump seat in front of him and slid onto it. I'm quite tall, so I sat with my elbows resting on my knees, my right hand clutching my left wrist. I'm sure that my face showed just how puzzled and curious I was.

The cheapest, most effective way to connect with others is to look them in the eye.

Muldoon was looking out the window at the drizzle falling on the people coming out of the subway station at Marble Arch. He turned to face me and adjusted the way he was sitting, then he grinned enthusiastically and looked me straight in the eye. He held up a finger. "Muldoon's

Rule Number One: *When you meet someone, look them in the eye and smile.*" He nodded once, and waited for me to acknowledge. I nodded back. Up came a second finger. "Muldoon's Rule Number Two: *When you want them to feel like they already know you, be a chameleon.*" I frowned. He caught it and changed the two fingers into a full hand, indicating I should wait, then reduced it to three fingers. "Muldoon's Rule Number Three: *Capture the imagination, and you capture the heart.*"

I sat back. I could tell he hadn't finished. He sat back as well.

"How many times a day do you deal with people who don't acknowledge your presence—who don't look at you?"

"Dozens, I suppose," I replied.

"Dozens of wasted opportunities. The single cheapest, easiest, and most effective way to maximize the connection between yourself and other people—your customers, colleagues, the receptionist back there, this cabdriver—is to look them in the eye and smile. Do you know why?"

"Because it says you are honest and interested in them." I had a feeling as soon as I said it that this wasn't going to be enough.

"Yes, good, very good. But there's more to it than that. How seriously would you take your favorite TV newscaster if he delivered the nightly news with his head down, reading off printed notes or looking out the window?"

"I don't think I'd take him very seriously." That seemed pretty obvious.

"And his message?"

"I'd probably lose interest unless I was forcing myself."

"Your message goes where your voice goes, and your voice goes where your eyes send it. How do you feel when you meet someone and they don't give you eye contact? How do you feel when they *do?* How do you feel when you are talking with someone and his or her eyes make contact with someone or something else?"

Eye contact is one of the most important nonverbal channels we have for communication. We've all heard that the eyes are the "windows to the soul," but they are also the windows to the sale. That's because eye contact sends the unconscious signal that trust is in the air. The eyes also answer critical questions when we're trying to connect: Is he paying attention to what I'm saying? Does this person find me attractive? Does this person like me? In social and workplace situations, subtle differences in eye contact can speak volumes. For example, when someone's eyes are narrowed and his head lowered and turned slightly to one side, and he is still maintaining eye contact, that can signal an invitation to discuss something very private, even intimate. The eyes can signal a feeling of superiority (when the head is raised) or hostility (when

EXERCISE

Eye Color

For one day, make a mental note of the color of the eyes of every person you meet. You don't have to remember the color, just take notice. That's it. Couldn't be simpler. Yet this simple exercise alone will massively increase self-confidence, eye contact, and rapport skills without your doing anything intimidating.

An amusing variation of this exercise to build rapport with customers is to tell your frontline staff you are doing a survey to find out if you serve more blue-eyed or brown-eyed customers, and just watch them hop to it. This works wonders in restaurants, banks, and hotels.

There's even a version of this for kids. It involves a small bribe—excuse me, reward. Tell your children you'll give them two bucks, or an extra hour at the pool hall, or a trip to Paris, or whatever if they come home from school tomorrow and tell you the eye color of all their teachers.

a gaze is level and unwavering). Conversely, looking away can imply weakness and avoidance. So, when you are discussing something that's important to you, be aware of what your eyes are telling your audience.

Muldoon looked straight into me and spoke softly and slowly: "Eyes radiate authority and give direction and focus and meaning to your message." He stared me down. I looked away. "Got it?" he inquired.

"Yes." I nodded vigorously.

"Well, smile then," he said. I faked a grin. "What's that?" he asked.

"I can't smile on demand," I said.

"A vanity case, are you? Afraid you'll look silly?"

"Stupid, more like," I said.

"Well, you'd better learn," he said. "The eyes aren't the only social cue we have to offer. The quickest way to put your best face forward is with a smile. Smile and the world smiles with you. Smile and you're saying, 'I'm approachable,' 'I'm happy,' and, 'I'm confident.' You can't afford to let vanity get in the way of success."

I'd known him for only three days, but in those three days I'd seen Francis Xavier Muldoon stir up a sales team, talk strategic planning with the editorial staff, and make a sale in ninety seconds. But now, motoring back to the office in the cab, it seemed like I'd known him all my life. The reason: Muldoon's Rule Number Two.

"How do you feel?" he asked.

"Good," I answered, and he raised his eyebrow slightly. "No, actually I feel terrific."

"I know," he said, then continued. "Do you know how I know?"

"I'm grinning and nodding and learning great stuff. It's obvious."

EXERCISE

How to Smile

The quickest way to put your best face forward is with a smile. Smiles signal approachability, happiness, and confidence. Professional models have tricks to help them get in the mood and smile. Here's my favorite. Put your face about ten inches in front of a mirror. Look yourself right in the eye and say the word "great" in as many different ways as you can: angry, loud, soft, sexy, like Jerry Lewis. . . . Keep going. Eventually you'll crack up. Repeat the exercise once a day for three days.

The next time you're going to meet someone, say "great" under your breath three times and you'll be smiling.

"Yes, but there's more to it than that. Look how you're sitting." I gazed down. I was leaning against the side of the cab with my right shoulder, my arms folded, and my chin almost touching my left collarbone.

"Now look how I'm sitting." I hadn't been aware of it before, but now that he'd drawn my attention to it, I saw that he was sitting in exactly the same way I was. I could have been looking in a mirror.

"Do you know what people do when they get along well, from a behavioral point of view?" I decided it was best just to shake my head as if to say no. He did the same: just shook his head as if to say no. "They become like each other. They start to sit the same way and talk in the same tone of voice. Today at the mail-order house, when the client tilted his head, mine tilted a little too. When he showed tension, I showed tension. When he relaxed, I relaxed. I changed my behaviors, attitudes, and expressions to suit the demands of the occasion—all to fit in."

"Like a chameleon?"

"And right now I'm doing the same with you—and you never consciously noticed. Even so, it made you feel comfortable and relaxed."

"That's why it seemed like you knew each other," I said. I was catching on.

Muldoon was right. We instinctively know how to fit in. We know how to be chameleons because we've been doing it all our lives. We learn by copying. If I smile at you, it's human nature for you to smile back. In much the same way, if I say "Good morning," there's a strong chance you'll respond in kind. This is a function of our natural predisposition to synchronize and reciprocate behavior. It's called limbic synchrony, and it's hardwired into the human brain.

As we grow and develop, our behavior is influenced by those around us. We learn our social graces by copying the manners of those with whom we eat and socialize. Rhythms are synchronized, behaviors are synchronized, and even knowledge is synchronized. When we see someone copying what we do, it can be flattering. When we hear someone say something we've said, we're happy because we know they are learning what we intend them to learn. We like people who are like us. They have learned the same things we have, and it feels comfortable and familiar.

We have been synchronizing ourselves—responding to emotional and physical feedback—since birth. A baby's body rhythms are synchronized with her mother's, a toddler's moods are influenced by his playmates, a teenager aligns her tastes with her peers', and an adult's views and preferences become remarkably defined by his friends. We like and feel comfortable with people who *are* like us. When you say, "I like you," chances are that what you are really saying is, "I am like you."

We have been unconsciously synchronizing ourselves with others since birth. Now is the time to start doing it consciously.

Synchronizing makes us feel as if we're all cut from the same cloth, part of the same group. If someone is doing the same thing we are—acting, dressing, or speaking like us—our mind tells us that they *are* like us. Want the big picture? You don't shout in church or whisper at a ball game. It's that simple: We are most successful when we adapt ourselves to the occasion.

Muldoon was telling me that when we consciously adapt our behaviors, attitudes, and expressions to the people we meet, they feel comfortable. We seem familiar, and so they like us.

Today, the people most likely to get ahead are the ones who get to know and understand lots of people within their company and their industry or business. They create diverse networks within their company because they connect to so many people that they become almost indispensable. These are the people who get promoted, not necessarily because they're doing the best work but because their work is widely known and their contributions are so broadly recognized. These are the chameleons.

Rush hour was upon us. Our cab was at a standstill and it looked like it would be at least another half hour before we got back to the office. It was getting dark.

"Are you hungry?" Muldoon asked.

"No, not remotely." I wasn't interested in food right now because I wanted to hear more. I was waiting to hear more about Rule Number Three. Muldoon suddenly turned and pointed out the back window. "Can you see that huge, old-fashioned streetlamp on the corner of that brick building?" I had to crouch a little, but I saw it.

"What about it?" I asked.

"I was there last night. That's Bentleys; it's a favorite after-work watering hole for journalists and advertising folk. I had dinner there with a couple of friends. The food's fabulous.

"To start, I ordered the spinach soufflé, with anchovy sauce drizzled into the center. It came with warm chunks of homemade bread. The bread was crunchy and the soufflé melted in my mouth. For the main course I had a peppercorn steak with creamy mashed potatoes and baby peas. To finish, I had the crêpes Suzette with an excellent vintage brandy."

Who said I wasn't hungry? Two minutes ago I wasn't, but now I was starving. I wanted that steak and mash so badly I was drooling. The more I thought about it, the more I wanted it. I could see it, hear it, feel it, taste it, and smell it.

"I think you just convinced me—I'm hungry!"

"No, I just played with your imagination to trigger your emotions—or in this case, your appetite." He smiled.

A light went on in my head. "The same way our client's imagination was triggered! When we dropped the huge sack of envelopes on his floor, he could imagine his dreams of successful advertising coming true."

Muldoon just nodded, then reached over and lifted his briefcase onto his lap. I thought he was going to show me something, but he just took out a slim folder and began to study what was inside it.

Riding backward in the cab's jump seat wasn't doing much to help my rumbling stomach, and anyway I'm well over six feet tall and the jump seat was not made for tall guys. After a minute or so, I waddled over to my original seat, next to him. He was completely engrossed, so I slid down in the seat, stretched out my legs, and stared out the window.

I glanced at Muldoon and wondered, What's the rest of his life like? Here's a guy who must be twice my age—I was almost twenty-one—who can probably turn his hand to anything. He's confident, he's calm, and he's charming. Everything he says seems so obvious—how come I never thought of it before? *Of course* you feel validated and connected when people look you in the eye. *Of course* you feel comfortable, connected, and respectful with people who are just like you. And without any doubt at all, the imagination is the key to the emotions. After all, the imagination is where most of us live—when we're not imagining the future, we're fantasizing about the past.

The glass partition separating us from the driver suddenly slid open. "Sorry, guvs. Looks like there's been a punch-up or something up in front. Shouldn't take long now, though."

"Thanks for the news," I said sarcastically.

"Not my fault, guv." The driver slammed the partition shut. The cabbie was right. It wasn't his fault. My stomach was making me cranky.

"That's fine, thanks for letting us know," Muldoon said loudly as he shot me a pained expression.

"Nice first impression. What do you want from the man—confrontation or cooperation?" It was clear that Muldoon had at least one more lesson to teach tonight. "What do you think will get us there faster—your treating him with respect or threatening to beat his brains out?"

"It's okay," he said, chuckling at the embarrassment written all over my face.

"Sooner or later, every successful person realizes that to get what you want from other people, they have to *want* to help you. There are only six ways you can get people to do things: by law, with money, by emotional force, physical force, the lure of physical beauty, or by persuasion. Of these, persuasion is the most efficient—it's the next level in the game. Work it out for yourself. Persuasion is more powerful, frequently quicker, usually cheaper, and yields more effective results than legal pressure, financial indulgence, emotional duress, physical force, or beauty. The problem is that if you blow your first impression, as you just did, you take persuasion off the table. You'll end up having to resort to one of those other ways to take control of the situation. The cabbie doesn't like you now, and he'll lump you in with all the other jerks who talk to cabbies like that."

Sir Winston Churchill called persuasion "the worst form of social control except for all the others." Aristotle posited that for persuasion to be truly effective, three elements must be present: trust, logic, and emotion. In modern terms that means that to be convincing, you need to make a good first impression by establishing trust through attitude (body language, voice tone) and personal packaging; you have to present your case with indisputable logic; and you've got to give a tug to the emotions to complete the process. It doesn't matter whether you're selling advertising space, recommending the Pinot Noir over the Burgundy, or giving the State of the Union address. You must make your audience trust you, you must make sense, and you've got to move them. To be convincing, you must communicate all that—and do it quickly.

But what exactly do we mean by communication? If I want one of my suppliers to do something for me by a certain date and they don't do it, then my communication has failed. Am I 100 percent responsible for whether my communication succeeds or fails? Yes. In business and life, the measure of effective communication lies in the response it gets. So, what do I do if my supplier fails to deliver

Defining what you want is the critical first step in almost any situation.

the goods? I could ask him what happened, and he could promise not to let it happen again. But what if he fails again? I could ask more often, or rant and rave, or plead. Or I could change what I do, do something different—even change suppliers. Then, if I don't get my desired outcome, I could change my tack again until I got what I wanted. Futility is doing the same thing over and over and expecting different results.

Here's a fact of life: All behavior is a feedback loop. You want something, you try for it. If you fail, you can try the same thing again; or you can figure out what the first try taught you (feedback), redesign your strategy, and then try again. Get more feedback from your second try, and keep changing and refining until you get what you want. Try and refine, try and refine. There is no failure, only feedback. The formula then becomes: Know what you want (in *positive* terms—"I want collaboration," not "I don't want squabbling"), find out what you're getting, and change what you're doing until you get what you want.

"See that sign over there?" Muldoon said, pointing out the side window at a Kentucky Fried Chicken restaurant. "Just look inside; it's packed. They have outlets all over the world, and they are successful because they have convinced people to go there to eat. They are a global brand because they deliver predictable nourishment conveniently and at fair value—and they keep their promise. The very nature of branding is that you make a promise to your customers and you keep it."

"And once they have you by the imagination, they've got you?"

"Exactly. By convincing, but not by coercion or intimidation. They never force anyone to eat there. Coercion is about getting people to do what you want them to; convincing is about getting them to *want* to do what you want them to do. It's how you tap into people's dreams and link your products or services or causes to the realization of their dreams—it's how you make them see it, hear it, feel it, and want it." Muldoon was on a roll. This was all great, but my hunger pangs were back again.

He paused and looked around for a moment. "See that restaurant back there?" We'd hardly moved in the last five minutes.

"Yes?"

"Look at it. It will help you remember the three aspects of successful communication. *KFC—know* what you want, *find out* what you're getting, and *change* what you do until you get what you want."

I knew precisely what I wanted right now—food—and staring at a chicken restaurant wasn't helping. Why was he doing this to me?

"Okay, I'm looking, but I have to say I don't see how it's going to help me."

But suddenly I got it: Muldoon was testing me. He'd made me hungry on purpose by cranking up my imagination. Then he'd pointed out a restaurant and told me that it was clean and convenient. Then he told me to know what I want, find out what I'm getting, and change what I do until I get what I want. And now he's waiting to see what I'll do about it.

"Mr. Muldoon."

"Frank."

"Frank, I'm starving."

He grinned. "I know. So, what are you going to do about it?"

I turned to look through the windshield—we were jammed right in the middle of the rush-hour traffic. We weren't going to make it back to the office before closing. When I turned back to Muldoon, he tugged up on the door handle and pushed it open with his elbow. "See you tomorrow." He stayed put.

This was my moment of truth, and logic and emotion at the very least were on my side. I grinned my biggest goofy grin, collected the bag of envelopes, and stepped past him out into the real world. Before he closed the door, he beckoned me closer with an Irish twinkle in his eye. I leaned forward and rain ran down my neck, but I kept on grinning. "Today I taught you technique. Next time I'll teach you substance. You've done well."

The traffic cleared and the cab pulled away. At that moment, only one thought went through my mind: I'd have gladly traded the pepper steak and mash for an umbrella and a raincoat. My dinner that night was fried chicken, lots of it.

Many years later I had cause to think back to that moment in the warm rain among the lights of London, when I was famished yet brimming with enthusiasm and overflowing with "The Gospel According to Muldoon." It was when I read in *The Wall Street Journal* one morning that Kentucky Fried Chicken had changed its name to KFC.

K: Know what you want.

F: Find out what you're getting.

C: Change what you do until you get what you want.

Do you know what you want? In the movie *Wall Street,* Charlie Sheen's character, Bud Fox, has had it with his situation as a stockbroker with his back always against the wall. So he figures out what he does want: power, riches, and excitement. He thinks that if he can land the ruthless financier Gordon Gekko's account, life will be perfect. He sets about getting an appointment, only to be turned down flat by Gekko's secretary. Instead of trying harder, louder, and more belligerently, he changes what he's doing and focuses, for a while, on softening her up with gifts and sweet talk. When that doesn't work, he changes what he's doing again, this time studying Gekko in such detail that he can almost read Gekko's mind. Then he connives a few moments alone with Gekko in a public place and makes him an offer he can't resist. It pays off. He ends up working for Gekko and getting what he wants. In this case, though, he gets far more than he wants. Nevertheless, *KFC* worked for him.

Unless you put *KFC* to work, you'll continue to get what you've always been getting.

Whether you're a dentist or a heavy-metal singer, a Realtor or the world's biggest manufacturer of feather mattresses, an enterprising MBA student or a fund-raiser for a small community church school, unless you put *KFC* to work for you, you'll keep on getting what you've always been getting. And those who do understand the principles of *KFC* will zoom right past you.

The directors of a small elementary school in Ontario wanted to move out of the church basement they'd been borrowing and into a building of their own. They'd held fund-raisers before, but those hadn't amounted to much, and were dependent on support mainly from the students' families and alumni. Next, they tried silent

EXERCISE

Do You Know What You Want?

Here's something you can try at work.

Notice three small, concrete things you don't like, or don't want to happen, at your workplace. ***I don't want to overhear other people on the phone, because it's distracting. I can't handle it when I don't get consensus at marketing meetings. I don't like it when customers are impatient.*** Now take your problem—the negative—and imagine it as a positive desire. ***I want a quiet place to work where I can concentrate. I want to learn more about what motivates my colleagues. I want to instill calm in other people.***

Once you know what you want, be creative and flexible and try out possible solutions. If overhearing other people is distracting, get a headset and earplugs. If that doesn't work, pinpoint who distracts you most and negotiate some repositioning. If that doesn't work, tell your boss you'll be more productive in a quiet environment and see what she can do. Get all the feedback you can, and on the basis of that, change what you do until you get what you want.

auctions—selling off goods and services solicited from local businesses—but they still weren't raising enough money. Out of tried-and-true ideas, they decided to change what they had been doing and try something completely

EXERCISE

How Will You Know When You've Got It?

Close your eyes and create a "future memory." Pick a specific and reasonable moment in time. What will it look like, sound like, feel like, smell like, and taste like? You'll learn later in the book that the raw language of the brain comes from the senses—pictures, sounds, and feelings. The infinite organizing power of your subconscious mind can better serve you when it can see, hear, and feel what you want, rather than being programmed with abstract, unspecific verbal goals. After all, which would work better—saying "I want happiness," or "I'll be happy and more productive when it's quiet where I work"? The latter, of course. It's much easier and more effective to show your subconscious what you mean by telling it specifically how achieving your goal will look, sound, and feel.

different. The fund-raising committee enlisted the help of some local professionals—entrepreneurs, a PR agency, a golfer, and a few merchants—to look at their options. At the meeting they decided how much money they wanted and what was reasonable to expect. They decided that their goal would be $25,000 in the first year, and at least $3,000 more per year for the next ten years.

What came out of the meeting was the school's first annual golf tournament. They wanted it not only to raise money but also to make enough of a splash that more people would become aware of the school. So, they called it Whole-in-One Golf Tournament, highlighting the school's mission—to educate the whole child—as well as the tournament. They knew they wouldn't succeed if this were just another golf tournament, so they figured out how to make it look unique and professional, rather than like a glorified bake sale. They convinced the captain of the fire department and the police chief to take part. But these two distinguished gents weren't enough to generate big-time interest, so they, in turn, convinced some of the local celebrities, including a famous rock musician who lived in the area, to take part. When twelve local merchants each offered prizes worth a minimum of a thousand dollars to anyone who got a hole in one, the fund-raisers knew that they'd made it.

From the day they started fund-raising, this group knew what they wanted; over the years, they found out what they were getting; and they changed what they were doing until they got what they wanted. Because they adhered to the *KFC* model, the tournament exceeded its goals in the first year. The directors gained feedback from the event and are already looking at a promising "second annual event."

90-Second Summary

"The Gospel According to Muldoon"

First impressions set the tone for success more than any other factor.

- **Look people in the eye and smile.** Your message goes where your voice goes, and your voice goes where your eyes send it. Eye contact engenders trust. Smiling makes you appear happy and confident. Say "great" to yourself three times and get in the mood.

- **Fit in—become a chameleon.** We feel comfortable and relaxed with people who are like us. Synchronize your body language with others' to achieve an immediate connection.

- **Capture the imagination and you capture the heart.** Use sensory-rich language and images so others can see, hear, feel, and sometimes even smell and taste what you mean.

Being Convincing

Convincing is about getting others to *want* to do what you want them to do. For it to be effective, three elements must be present: a trusting first impression, indisputable logic, and a tug at the emotions.

- **Trust.** Trust can precede you implicitly in your title ("general manager"), your credentials, or your reputation. It is earned at first contact through attitude (body language, voice tone) and personal packaging.
- **Logic.** Your position, presentation, or point must make sense.
- **Emotion.** Your argument must appeal to the imagination, and thus to the emotions.

Appeal to all three levels so the person, group, or audience feels: *I trust you, you make sense, and you move me.* Trust must come first.

KFC

The meaning of communication lies in the response it gets. You are 100 percent responsible for whether your communication succeeds or fails. ***KFC*** is the formula for successful communication.

- ***K*: Know what you want.** Define what you want in positive terms, and preferably in the present tense.
- ***F*: Find out what you're getting.** Pay attention to all the feedback you get and learn from it so you can determine what is moving you toward your goal and what is distracting you from it.

- ***C*: Change what you do until you get what you want.** It's futile to do the same thing over and over and expect different results. If you don't get what you want, try different approaches, sometimes radically different, until you do get what you want.

Part Two

The New Rules: Connecting with Human Nature

Every time you say hello to a stranger, the person unconsciously decides whether to run, fight, or stay. Dozens of snap judgments are made in a flash, at the subconscious level. You've heard people say, "I knew I liked her the moment I met her." But how does this all happen?

It happens because it's part of the original wiring of the human animal. Once the "like"/"dislike" filters are set up, everything else is influenced by the initial instants of every encounter: If I like you, I see the best in you, and you can do no wrong. But if I don't like you, there's nothing you can do right.

We can't stop people from making snap judgments, but we can make those judgments work in our favor. This section deals with the new rules. They build on what Muldoon taught me, what scientists and experts have told me, and what eyes-wide-open wonder and curiosity have shown me to be true. Here you'll learn how to adjust your nonverbal signals to make the other person feel comfortable, safe, and trusting with you the moment they set eyes on you.

2
Neutralize the Fight-or-Flight Response

The first few seconds of an initial encounter between two people are driven by instinctive reactions. Each person makes unconscious, unthinking appraisals that center around their safety: "I do/don't feel safe with you," "I do/don't trust you."

The animal instinct for survival makes us superalert at a subconscious level on first contact, and for a split second, as the body enters a heightened state of awareness, a mental shield goes up to protect it. As you peer out from behind this shield, you decide just how much it's safe to reveal—and how fast you are prepared to reveal it. The impressions formed at this stage can set the mood and color of expectations, and rev up the imagination to make snap judgments—right or wrong—about the person we're encountering.

But take heart. You can neutralize the fight-or-flight response in others and encourage favorable snap judgments, and thereby establish a receptive mood and positive expectations. To start with, what do you think is the number-one trait that people unconsciously admire in others? First and foremost, they are drawn toward individuals who look healthy and vital, people who are putting out energy into the room, rather than those who are sucking it in. People seek out those who will encourage their growth, those who are giving rather than taking.

If there's one thing that suggests health and vitality, it's positive energy, which can be projected in the way you come into a room, the way you occupy your space in the room, and the way you give attention to what others have to say. Attitude, posture, facial expressions, and eye contact influence the energy you radiate, and the people you encounter are passing judgment on what you're putting out every second of the day.

Dr. Nalini Ambady of Harvard University made a stunning discovery during a study of the nonverbal aspects of good teaching. After videotaping hundreds of classroom hours, Dr. Ambady showed one group of students a two-second clip of unfamiliar teachers with the sound turned off. Then she gave this group, as well as a second group of students who had spent an entire semester studying under these same teachers, a checklist of educational attributes and asked them to rate the teachers. Both sets of students came to almost identical conclusions about the teachers, thus demonstrating the power of first impressions.

The following checklist (not one used by Dr. Ambady) lists a few of the nonverbal signals that people give off, causing others to make snap judgments about them. There are many more, but this will give you an idea of why your nonverbal impact is so important. If you're reading this book in a restaurant, or in an airport, or in any other public place, look at the strangers around you and rate them on any of the criteria. Circle the number you feel best describes the person you are rating. For example, circle 5 if the person looks very *talkative,* 2 if the person seems somewhat *silent.*

Silent	**1**	**2**	**3**	**4**	**5**	**Talkative**
Closed	**1**	**2**	**3**	**4**	**5**	**Open**
Dull	**1**	**2**	**3**	**4**	**5**	**Interesting**
Undependable	**1**	**2**	**3**	**4**	**5**	**Reliable**
Composed	**1**	**2**	**3**	**4**	**5**	**Excitable**
Flighty	**1**	**2**	**3**	**4**	**5**	**Persistent**
Reserved	**1**	**2**	**3**	**4**	**5**	**Friendly**
Careful	**1**	**2**	**3**	**4**	**5**	**Adventurous**
Not Jealous	**1**	**2**	**3**	**4**	**5**	**Jealous**
Unscrupulous	**1**	**2**	**3**	**4**	**5**	**Scrupulous**

As you score these strangers, you are rating, or responding to, the nonverbal messages they are giving off. And you may be completely wrong! Unfortunately, many of us unknowingly send out signals through our body language and our personal packaging (style, dress, demeanor) that cause the people we encounter to misjudge us before we've even opened our mouths. Yes, everyone does judge books by their covers, restaurants by the photos on the menu, and frequently, cities or even whole cultures by the first person they encounter at the airport! But you can learn how to beat this rush to judgment.

People can't stop making snap judgments about others. It's human nature to do so. But you can neutralize the fight-or-flight response and further your chances of making a trusting connection.

Shortly after the publication of my first book, *How to Make People Like You in 90 Seconds or Less,* a reporter from the *Houston Chronicle* decided that rather than interview me, he'd put me to the test.

Out we went onto the streets of downtown Houston—the reporter, a photographer, and I. The plan was this: The reporter would decide whom I would approach. Then he and the photographer would hide around the corner and watch what happened.

"See that group over there? Go and make them like you,"

EXERCISE

Snap Judgments

- Try this at a function, a trade show, or in the grocery store line—somewhere you encounter strangers you can approach. Pick out a person you think has some of the negative aspects in the list on page 43, ask them where something is—the rest room or the deli—and check out their response to see how valid your evaluation was. Repeat the exercise with someone exhibiting the positive aspects and see if they match up to your expectations. In both cases, try to pinpoint what you saw in the other person that led you to this evaluation.
- Look at some of your office mates and try to evaluate them as if it were the first time you were seeing them. Does this I've-never-seen-you-before evaluation agree with what you know about this person? What does this tell you about the way you typically evaluate people on first sight?
- Dig out some photos of yourself, old and recent, and see what cues you were and are giving off. Figure out what they tell you about your personality and relationships at the time they were taken. This will help you become sensitized to what you are communicating through your appearance and the effect that has on how you connect with others.

the reporter instructed. I had already explained to him that the book is not about blindsiding people in public; nobody likes that. "Nevertheless," he said, "it makes a good story."

Straight into the deep end: five bicycle couriers having their lunch. Over I go, wearing a double-breasted blazer, a white button-down shirt, black jeans, and red shoes. Within ten seconds we're having a great time, all chatting away like pals. I called the reporter out of his hiding place and he came over with the photographer and asked everybody whether they liked me or not. Here's what the messengers said: "He seemed like a nice guy." "He didn't seem threatening." "When I saw his red shoes, I thought he was cool." "He spoke well and was dressed well." "I felt comfortable with him."

We moved along and the reporter upped the ante. An expensively dressed businesswoman came rushing out of a building carrying a briefcase and heading for the building across the road. "Her," said the reporter. "Make her like you." "Thanks a lot," I replied as I walked briskly to intercept her. Twenty seconds later we were laughing, and she was chatting away happily. "He was very warm," she told the reporter. "He connected mostly by looking me in the eye. I could tell he was listening and responded back. And he smiled."

The reporter decided to increase the degree of difficulty: two bicycle patrolmen from the Houston Police

Department, sitting in front of a bus stop. Similar results. "He didn't come across as someone I should distrust," said one officer. "He was dressed decently and came up in a mannerly way. He didn't appear to be threatening," said the other. "But did you like him?" asked the reporter. "Sure, he was a nice guy."

About a month after the story appeared, I got a call from a well-known columnist at *The New York Times,* who said, "It might work in those other places, but this is New York."

He put me through the wringer, throwing everything at me from an attractive, annoyed-looking young woman alone in Grand Central Station to the famously rude (it's a bluff) waiters at the Carnegie Deli to a woman who sells tokens down in the subway, and more. The results were always the same—I connected 100 percent of the time.

So how come? What was I doing? And why do I believe that just because I can make people feel comfortable, relaxed, and ready to step out from behind the shield in ninety seconds or less, that anyone can?

Here's what I took into consideration, and you've read enough by now to do the same.

In every one of these situations, I first asked myself, What do I want? This is supremely important. I wanted the individual I approached to trust me. With that in mind, the question that made sense for me to ask a complete stranger in a situation with zero context was: "When you meet someone for the first time, how can you tell if you trust them?" (By zero context I mean that if you're in a station, you can ask questions about trains, or in a pharmacy, about headache pills. Those are all questions that are safe and sensible in those locales. But if I had done that, it would have been phony, and the person would sense it and keep the shield up. I wanted my question to be intriguing, non-threatening, and appropriate to the situation.)

Before I set out, I packaged myself carefully to appear honest, vibrant, and healthy. My look works *for me*. You must find your own signature look (more on this on page 154). What works for me is:

> *Authority from the waist up.* Double-breasted blazer with expensive brass buttons; starched white button-down-collar shirt.
>
> *Approachability from the waist down.* Clean, new black jeans. They are less formal than dress pants, and I like them. Bright red, shiny, expensive leather shoes—a little offbeat, showing I don't take myself too seriously.

Here's what I did (and what you can do) to make a great first impression:

- First, as I've mentioned, I was dressed in a calculated combination of authority and approachability.

- Before I approached anyone, I adjusted my attitude. I was *curious,* with a dash of *playful.* As I approached each encounter, I recalled a time when I felt the combination of curious and playful, and that got me in the mood (see page 68 for more on this).
- As I approached each encounter, I said to myself, "Great, great, great," and that made me smile. (You can say it out loud or in your head; the important thing is to get the feeling. Just the word itself is upbeat and encouraging.)
- The minute I walked up, I took note of the color of the person's eyes.
- I turned my body as if to point my heart at the person's heart (for more on this, see page 72). This move demonstrates open body language and an open heart.
- I let them see I had nothing threatening in my hands. You don't want to go triggering the fight-or-flight mechanism. I carry an expensive-looking, closed fountain pen in my hand as a prop. It's the next best thing to a lab coat, and its expensive look gives me an air of authority. The fact that it's closed means I'm probably not going to write anything down (as in make a report).
- I asked a softening question as soon as I walked up. In every case I said, "Excuse me, can I ask you a question?" Then I asked my real question: "When you meet

someone for the first time, how can you tell if you trust them?" It was easy to look and sound interested in the answer because I was. (Prepare your question ahead of time—know what you want.)

- Finally, I began immediately to synchronize my body language and tone of voice with theirs (for more on this, see page 73). When I spoke to more than one person, as was the case with the bike couriers, I turned toward each of them in turn and adjusted my overall stance to match theirs.

At the beginning of any new encounter you have to do several things at the same time. The eight stages I just listed probably took no longer than ten seconds, during which I was talking, observing, and responding. What you communicate in the opening moments of an encounter establishes you either as a credible, honest, vibrant, and healthy individual or as one who causes others to walk away.

As soon as the piece came out in *The New York Times, Good Morning America* decided to see if I was the only person who could connect with people in ninety seconds or less, or if this was something that could be learned by anyone who picked up my book. Lara Spencer, one of the anchors, took to the streets of New York City armed with the book and tried it out for herself. Success rate: 100

percent! Then she persuaded a passerby, a robust-looking fellow in his late thirties, dressed in a T-shirt and jeans, to give it a try. After five minutes' training with the book, he had the same results. And so will you.

Living Up to Expectations

In business, first impressions are frequently colored by expectations. We expect people to live up to the image we have created in our minds from what they have said, or from how they've said it, in nonvisual media—say by phone, letter, or e-mail. Once we do see them, we expect them to look the part. When they don't live up to these expectations, we tend to be somewhat disappointed, and this disappointment can make us see less than the best in the person. On the other hand, when they meet or exceed our expectations, we are prepared to give more, listen harder, and invest added optimism.

We can't stop ourselves or others from making snap judgments—they are part of humans' inborn, instinctive fight-or-flight response. But we can learn to see beyond what meets the eye and avoid making the mistakes that go along with that sort of arbitrary decision making. Any time you are diverted by someone or something not meeting your expectations, stop and refocus. Ask yourself, What do I want?

Be aware of your perceptions and try to make sure they are not getting in the way of doing business.

Eddie, a print broker, hadn't yet met the creative director for one of his newer accounts, though they'd had a phone and e-mail relationship for a few months. When they met for lunch for the first time, here's what happened in the initial twenty seconds:

Eddie's eyes popped when he got his first glimpse of Pierre. The man wasn't at all what he'd expected. For starters, Pierre had to be at least six and a half feet tall, and his hair was buzzed up another inch on top of that. Eddie's job was all about keeping his shop moving—getting the clients to make a decision *fast,* have their materials in *fast,* and pay their bills *fast.* Most of the people he worked with were little guys—*fast* guys. What am I going to do with the Jolly Green Giant? he unconsciously thought. Anybody or anything that slows us down hurts us.

Even before Pierre offered him a hand to shake, Eddie was leaping to a host of conclusions about Pierre based on his looks. And none of them were going to help these two men make a connection. By the time they got to their table in the restaurant, Eddie had convinced himself that he and Pierre could not work together, and he was probably going to have to write off this account.

I guess the company wouldn't have given him this position if he couldn't do the job, Eddie thought, but he didn't find this thought all that comforting.

How can Eddie get past this sort of first impression, in which his expectation has turned out to be quite counter to what he's presented with? How can he communicate openly with Pierre? Stop right there! Eddie's problem isn't about communicating with Pierre; it's about communicating with himself. Eddie is focusing on Pierre's physical appearance rather than his talent. He has lost sight of what he wants—a creative director who doesn't cause problems for his printers, who doesn't cause problems by slowing everything and everybody down. Right now, Eddie has no idea whether or not Pierre will do this—but he does have plenty of assumptions.

The same thing is true for the notions you may have in your own mind about people in the office that you see on a regular basis but whom you don't know well. The initial impact a person made—one, twelve, or forty-eight months ago—may still be affecting your perception of that person today. That long-ago misimpression may be keeping you from recognizing a potentially valuable resource. Remember, when you like someone, you see the best in them, but when you don't, you may see only the worst. Snap judgments set up filters in the mind, and everything about the person is judged through these filters. Put your

EXERCISE

Playing with Personal Space

Grab a friend, a colleague, or someone else you want to have some fun with and try this.

Stand about twenty feet apart, facing each other. Tell your friend that right now you are in her public space and you are going to walk toward her very slowly, and you want her to nod or say "Now" when you enter her social space. You should be able to anticipate her response just by watching her body language. Once she has let you know you're in her social space, continue slowly approaching and tell her to indicate when you've entered her personal space. Again, you'll probably be able to read it in her reactions. Finally, after she's let you know you

filters aside and look at the person again through gentler eyes, and you may be pleasantly surprised by what you've been missing.

Personal Space

One of the easiest mistakes to make during the first ninety seconds of any encounter is to misjudge how much the other person needs their personal space. A mistake here can trigger a truly deep-seated response.

are in her personal space, tell her to let you know when you reach her private space. Once again, this should be completely obvious by her reactions, and you will know at the same time she does.

Now reverse the roles. Let her do it to you.

The point of this exercise is to let you see, hear, and feel, in a very real way, that these invisible boundaries actually exist and are to be respected. Stepping into and out of personal and private space can have a similar effect on making and breaking synchronization when you want to evoke an emotional response in your favor.

Respect people's space. Unexpected intrusions are bad for rapport, especially if they come as a surprise.

A telephoto lens is like a telescope: It makes things look much closer than they are. You can fill a frame with a subject's face using a telephoto lens and still be fifteen feet away or so. Try to shoot the same full-frame portrait with a standard lens and you're going to be right in your subject's face—maybe two feet away! Does the shot look different? Yes, a little. Does it feel different? Yes, a lot.

When another person gets too close to us, that can trigger our own fight-or-flight response. We all understand that the farther away from us a person is, the less threatening they are. But what we're not always clear about is how our body and our feelings alter as people come closer to us.

Imagine this: A person is moving toward you, passing from your *public* space into your *social* space, then from your social space into your *personal* space. He just keeps coming. Doesn't your heart beat a little faster and your awareness of that person grow? Don't your other senses wake up as your body tries to figure out what he is about to do? The ultimate intrusion is when an uninvited guest invades your *private* space—that's when you may feel an uncontrollable urge to withdraw or to repel the intruder with physical or verbal reactions.

An unconscious invasion of someone's personal space can trigger a deep-seated response and cause real barriers to go up.

Sounds dramatic, doesn't it? In a bustling office, your body probably goes through some or all of this cycle a dozen times a day without your being fully aware of it. People are constantly ignoring cues and signals and coming closer than we'd like them to, or wandering too far away when we need them to hear or see us.

90-Second Summary

Neutralize the Fight-or-Flight Response

Encourage others to make favorable snap judgments about you. Establish a receptive mood and positive expectations.

- Be mindful of your body language and personal packaging. We are drawn to people who look healthy and vital. Attitude, posture, facial expressions, and eye contact all influence the energy you radiate. Find a signature look that inspires trust: a combination of authority and approachability.

- Adjust your attitude to fit the situation before you approach someone.

- Demonstrate open body language and signal an open heart: Smile, make eye contact, point your heart at the person's heart, and let it be seen that you have nothing to conceal in your hands—that you present no threat.

- Ask a softening question: "Excuse me, can I ask you a question?" "How can you tell . . . ?" "What do you think about . . . ?"

- Synchronize your body language and tone of voice. If you are dealing with a small group, synchronize with each individual as you turn to him or her.

Preconceived Expectations

We can't stop ourselves or others from making snap judgments about people, but we can learn to see beyond what meets the eye. Don't get lost in what a person looks or sounds like, or even old misconceptions of what you think they're like. Remember what you want, and stay focused on your outcome.

Personal Space

Respect people's space. Getting too close to another person can trigger their fight-or-flight response. Unexpected intrusions are bad for rapport, especially if they come as a surprise.

3

Work Your *ABC*: Attitude, Body Language, and Congruence

Last year I visited some thirty cities in an exhausting but exciting six-week business trip. One early afternoon I flew into a city I had never visited before. I stopped at the airport information desk to ask a question. The response was a grunt and a finger pointing me in the right direction. No eye contact and no courtesy—nothing. What a lousy setup for a famous city.

The next day I flew into St. Louis. Before the door to the aircraft opened, I looked out the window next to me and saw that the baggage handlers had already positioned the rolling conveyor up to the forward baggage hold. The luggage was starting to roll off our plane. There was a guy at the bottom of the conveyor who, as he picked up each bag, danced with it over to the cart. What a great attitude this guy had! He looked like he was having a great time (mind you, he could have been doing it to keep warm; it was winter), and that set me up for the city. This is fabulous, I said to myself. I like this place already.

What was I reacting to through the aircraft window? I didn't know the guy; I'd never seen him before, and for all I knew I'd never see him again. But something about this stranger who didn't even know I existed had touched me.

He'd gotten to me with *attitude*. Attitudes drive behavior. Before you say a word, they can infect the people who see you with the same behavior. Just as laughing, crying, and yawning are infectious, attitude is infectious. Somehow just by looking, I had been infected by this man's attitude, and it caused me to feel joy—without thinking.

The *ABC* of Nonverbal Communication: Attitude, Body Language, and Congruence

Your attitude is the first thing people pick up on in face-to-face communication. And just as you can consciously neutralize the fight-or-flight response, so you can control and adjust your attitude, *if you want to*. The key to communicating your attitude is body language and congruence.

EXERCISE

Attitudes Drive Behavior

This is an exercise in attitude adjustment. Take a few minutes to set aside your reservations, to prepare yourself for an imaginative journey down the halls of your office. Don't worry, we're not asking you to look foolish—you're going to look normal to your office mates. Ninety-nine percent of this exercise is going on inside your head. Show only enough of this behavior to remind yourself what's going on.

- One morning, imagine you are a hippopotamus. Take on the slow, rolling walk and deliberate stare of the hippo—get in a hippo mood, or attitude. Got it? Now walk around the office, greeting people as you go. Notice how it feels.
- The next day, imagine you are a kangaroo, bouncing around all peppy and intense. Put on a kangaroo attitude and greet some more people. Notice how this feels. How is it different from feeling like a hippo?
- Finally, imagine you are a cougar, sleek, prowling, supremely aware, and confident as you make your way to your office.

Did you notice a difference in how people responded to you? Did you radiate a different type of energy? Did people seem more energetic when you were a kangaroo? Did they talk a little slower when you were a hippo? Did they seem a little skittish, or even a bit jumpy, when you were a cougar?

Your mind and your body are one system—change one, and the other will follow. Stick out your tongue and put your hands on the side of your head and make those funny finger-wobbling antlers that kids do, and try to feel miserable at the same time. You can't do it; your body won't let you. Jump up and down on a trampoline at your neighborhood barbecue and try to be serious. Not possible; your body won't allow it. This is a massive oversimplification of the mind-body connection, but you get the point.

Before You Open Your Mouth

Turn on *The Tonight Show* and turn off the sound. Pretend you've never seen or heard Jay Leno before. Now tell me, is this guy funny? You laughed, didn't you? If not, I'll bet you smiled.

Why is this? How does it happen? The very first impression Jay Leno gives off comes from his deliberately playful body language. Because we have an inherent tendency to align ourselves with other people's attitudes, we start to feel the same way within the first couple of seconds of seeing him—even with the sound off.

Jay's body language is a result of his deliberately chosen mental attitude—he makes a conscious decision to act the way he does. The result is that his body sends out a message that everyone understands. This doesn't

Attitude Rundown

Really Useful Attitudes	*Really Useless Attitudes*
Warm	**Angry**
Enthusiastic	**Sarcastic**
Confident	**Impatient**
Supportive	**Bored**
Relaxed	**Disrespectful**
Obliging	**Arrogant**
Curious	**Pessimistic**
Resourceful	**Anxious**
Comfortable	**Rude**
Helpful	**Suspicious**
Engaging	**Vengeful**
Laid-back	**Afraid**
Patient	**Self-conscious**
Welcoming	**Mocking**
Cheery	**Embarrassed**
Interested	**Sneering**
Courageous	**Disheartened**

happen by accident. He chooses his attitude—he gets in the mood—before he goes on.

Anyone can do it if they want to. Maybe you've walked up to two people you know at work and realized, too late,

(continued on page 66)

EXERCISE

Three Attitude-Adjustment Games

Here are three games that will really drive home the point that a useful attitude makes all the difference.

Mirror Talk

As children we learn "pretend" games. As grown-ups we abandon this valuable social and cognitive learning tool. Happily enough, these games are still available to us. We are fantastic at pretending.

Try this. Stand in front of a mirror and say, "You drive me crazy."

Now, with as much body language as you can muster up, and with the appropriate voice tone for each attitude below, say the same phrase again and pretend you are

1. Angry 2. Brave 3. Happy 4. Humble 5. Calm

Same words—totally different meanings. What did you see, what did you hear, what did you feel? Now go through the list of attitudes again, saying, "I'm going home now."

Evaluate again. Did you notice how your body changed for each attitude? How your tone of voice altered each time you changed your attitude? When you adjust your attitude around other people, they pick up the same feelings you have and begin to experience them for themselves. How much sense does it make to be angry or impatient when you want to make a good first impression? How much better to be excited or warm?

Body Talk

Write down or, better still, remember these five attitudes: *angry, brave, happy, humble, calm.* The next time it's convenient, as you walk down a corridor, through a mall, or up a street, rotate your body language and feelings through these attitudes. Start off angry—walk, think, breathe, talk to yourself as if you are angry. After a certain distance, change quickly from being angry to being brave. After angry becomes brave, brave becomes happy, happy becomes humble, and humble becomes calm. The changeover can occur every five offices, every four stores, every block—it doesn't matter.

Notice how changing your attitude affects your posture, breathing, thoughts, facial expressions, heart rate, speed, stride, and so on. Notice how people passing by respond to you. If you feel a bit psycho doing this exercise, that's okay. But if the security guard throws you out of the mall, you're probably taking it further than you need to.

Winner and Loser

Set aside twenty-five minutes. For the first five minutes, act like a winner. Chest out, proud posture, confident breathing from the abdomen—imagine crowds on either side cheering you on as you smile at them. For the next five, act like a loser. Let your shoulders droop, feel miserable, put on the downcast eyes and the insecure glower. Next five like a winner again, then five more like a loser, and the final five like a winner. Which did you prefer? It helps to know what they both feel like, but when you're connecting in business, it goes without saying, always act like a winner.

that they're in the middle of a huge argument. You say hello. They look up at you and pretend that nothing's going on, smile, and say, "Bryant, how nice to see you." They chat pleasantly with you for a moment, and as soon as you excuse yourself and are out of sight, they go back at it.

There are two distinct classes of attitude: useful ones, which attract, and useless ones, which repel. *Resourceful, curious,* and *welcoming* are examples of the useful sort; *bored, hostile,* and *impatient* typify the other sort.

Take a look at the Attitude Rundown list on page 63. To get in the mood to connect in business in ninety seconds or less, you should choose a really useful attitude that feels right for you.

Look at the list and go over the words in the left-hand column. Slip into some of the attitudes that appeal to you. To do this, just close your eyes and think of a *specific moment in time* when you felt that way. Keep playing around until you find one that suits you. When you've got it, close your eyes again and relive what you saw, heard, and felt at the time (you can bring in smell and taste if they were part of it) in as much detail as you can. Bring on the pictures, the sounds, and the physical sensations. The brain is very good at unpacking sensory memories and letting you romp around and relive them. Take this attitude out for a good ride. Next, do the smile exercise ("Great, great, great") from page 20, rolling these two exercises together. Close your eyes again, pump up all the senses once more, and—when the pictures are big and colorful, the sounds clear and directional, and you can feel the physical sensations—hear your voice yelling "Great, great, great," in wild and audacious tones. That's what a really useful attitude should feel like.

You Can't Lead if You Can't Convince

Attitudes are real and they can be consciously chosen. It is through our attitudes that we train our emotions.

Let's look at someone who is going to have to pick the right attitude if she's going to have any chance to succeed. Her name is Erin and she is a team leader in her company's information technology department. Erin's team is in the dumps. For the last three months they've been asked to do more—and get more out of the company's computer system—with fewer resources. Now she has more bad news for her team—the company needs them to step up one more time. Her team is being asked to bring a new system online, and they're not going to get any new people to help.

Erin feels truly disheartened, and it's written all over her face. She knows that if she walks into the meeting with this expression on her face, things are going to go from bad to

Three Really Useful Attitudes

There are three really useful attitudes that successful leaders have in common: enthusiasm, curiosity, and humility. In the right combination, these three attitudes create an irresistible presence.

Be enthusiastic. Enthusiasm is hypnotic, magnetic, unstoppable. You can't buy it—you can only reveal it. It infects others with feelings of excitement, energy, and vitality. The word *enthusiasm* comes from the Greek, meaning "God flowing through."

Stay curious. Show me a businessperson who is hungry to learn more about what's going on

worse. She knows it's hard to hide how she feels, so she must change how she feels. She must change the really useless attitude of *disheartened* to a really useful one, but to which one, and how? What attitude does she need to convey when she joins the team in the conference room that will get them not only to meet but to beat this challenge? And how does she put it on before she goes in?

The last time she felt this way was two years ago, when she was out of work and beginning to doubt herself. One afternoon she was flicking through the TV channels and

around them and I'll show you someone who is evolving, moving forward, making connections. Always be open to your natural-born curiosity.

Embrace humility. Most successful people have large egos and a flair for self-promotion, yet manage to contain them and display a public persona rooted in modesty and service to others. When a large ego is generously wrapped in humility, it is a handsome package. An ego that's not tempered with humility is arrogant and ugly.

Think of any great leader you admire and you will find these three attitudes at the center of their success. Enthusiasm, curiosity, and humility can be consciously chosen behaviors. They can infuse you with unmistakable signals of vigor and openness.

she came across a program called *The Secrets of Talented Women.* Some really successful, famous women were discussing how they overcame obstacle after obstacle and over and over kept summoning up the courage to succeed. Something about the courageous attitude the women showed in these interviews rubbed off on her. She picked up something from them. She found herself walking into interviews and meetings with her back straight and a smile on her face, and not long after, she landed the job she has today. Now it was time to summon up her trusty friend, her really useful attitude called *courage,* once again.

Erin had been to one of my seminars and remembered a couple of the techniques that I'd taught for attitude adjustment. So she closed her door, sat down, and closed her eyes. Then, sitting quietly, she recalled a specific moment from her past when she was exploding with courage. She accessed what she saw through her eyes, heard through her ears, and felt throughout her body at that moment. Next, in her mind's eye she saw, heard, and felt herself in action and at her best. If I could do it then, Erin thought, I know I can do it now. Still sitting with her eyes closed, surrounded by what she was seeing clearly and hearing in detail, and with feelings of courage running through her body, Erin said to herself, "Great, great, great." And she felt and looked courageous and excited all over again.

Even when it feels as if the world is coming to an end, you can change your attitude from useless to useful.

Walking down the corridor to the meeting room, Erin was saying "great" in her head so many times and in so many wild and crazy voices that she wanted to yell it out with all her might so everyone could feel as powerful as she did. She strode into the room like a warrior. She looked like a leader, sounded like a leader, and spoke like a leader. Her team was infected by Erin's attitude. They got the job done.

Know What Your Body Is Saying

Volumes have been written about body language, but at the end of the day it mostly comes down to two things: What signals are you sending to others about yourself, and what emotional feedback are you giving others in response to the signals they are sending you? Body language accounts for more than half of what other people respond to and make assumptions about when connecting with you. And more often than not, you're not consciously thinking about it. By becoming conscious, you're 50 percent ahead of the game.

Open, or Closed?

Body language can be loosely broken into two kinds of signal: open and closed. Open body language exposes the heart and is welcoming, while closed body language defends the heart and appears standoffish and sometimes aloof. In other words, you're constantly saying either, "Welcome, I'm open for business," or, "Go away, I'm closed for business." You may be showing that you are an opportunity or a threat; a friend or a foe; confident or uncomfortable; telling the truth or spouting lies. I began this chapter with the section on attitude because when you are operating from inside a really useful attitude, your body language tends to take care of itself. Attitudes like enthusiasm, curiosity, and humility bring with them unmistakable signals of openness. Nonetheless, there are things you can consciously do to make sure you're showing your best face.

Open for Business

If you want to show that you're open for business, a friend and not a foe, without saying a word, you have to open yourself up to the world in the first seconds of every encounter. Open body language—together with open facial expressions—includes uncrossed arms and legs, ease in facing the person, good eye contact, smiling,

EXERCISE

Heart to Heart

For one day, point your heart at the heart of everyone you meet. This will demonstrate open body language and build trust and comfort. When another person's natural instincts ask "Friend or foe? Opportunity or threat?" you will come out on top.

standing or sitting erect, leaning forward, flexible shoulders, and a generally relaxed aura. Open body language makes expressive use of hands, arms, legs, and feet.

Holding Something In—Keeping People Out

Closed body and facial language, as you might expect, is the opposite. If your heart is turned away and your arms and legs are crossed defensively, and if you're hiding your hands, clenching your fists, avoiding eye contact, fidgeting nervously, and showing a tendency to move away—these are all things that signal discomfort, rejection, and apprehension. Closed body language exhibits reduced or awkward use of the limbs.

Let me add as a caveat that individual gestures, like individual words on this page, don't make much of a statement, but when two or more gestures combine, they begin to give a clear indication of how a person is feeling.

Synchronizing Body Language

People who are in rapport exhibit an interesting behavior characteristic: They unconsciously synchronize their body language and their vocal characteristics. And as F. X. Muldoon taught me, when you deliberately synchronize your body with another's, amazing connections can happen. Our response to synchronization is a

EXERCISE

Synchronize Body Language

For one day, synchronize the overall body language of the people you meet. This is the fastest way to build trust and communication. Don't go over the top. Do as little as you need to adjust to them.

We naturally synchronize our tone of voice and body language with our friends and people we trust. You can do it with anyone you choose.

Make and Break

Once you are good at it—one day should make you an expert—practice synchronizing for about thirty seconds, then break the synchronizing for thirty seconds, then make it again. Go through the cycle a few times.

Notice the difference. Does it feel as if there's a wall going up as you feel the trust disappear? Now get back in synch and feel the relief as it returns.

function of our predisposition to reciprocate behavior. It's hardwired into the human brain.

I mentioned this phenomenon in my first book, and during a radio interview the host told me, "I read your book over the weekend. On Sunday night my husband took me out to dinner, so I decided to try out your synchronizing exercise with someone in the restaurant to see what would happen. I was a little skeptical."

She went on to explain that sitting about three tables away was a slightly older couple. The woman was more or less facing in her direction, but they never made eye contact.

"For about twenty minutes I gently synchronized her overall body language and posture. When she moved, I moved; when she shifted her weight from one elbow to the other, I followed. I did it all without ever looking directly at her. And then an incredible thing happened. The woman got up from the table and came over to me. 'Excuse me,' she said, 'but I'm sure I know you.' I was blown away."

My host had learned how to be a chameleon, to affect someone's feelings and behavior—to make a connection—without ever saying a word. Imagine how much more effective you can be when you're face-to-face with clients and coworkers, friends and strangers, using all of the tools you possess to make a connection.

At the end of the exercises on synchronizing at one of my seminars, a young man asked if he could share a story with the hundred or so people in attendance. Earlier in the session he had been full of energy; now he looked very serious. All eyes were focused on him. He sat on the low windowsill and began. "I am from Brazil. One day about three years ago, I came home to find my sister sitting, holding a gun in her mouth. I was really scared. I didn't know what to do." He was breathing slowly, his eyes unfocused, as he told the story.

"We always had guns in the house. I don't know why, but I went and got a gun and sat down next to her. I was sitting just like her, like this." He showed us: knees together, elbows on his thighs, one hand near his mouth, the other gripping the wrist of that hand. "I had the gun in this hand." He flexed the hand that was close to his mouth. "I put my body in the same position as hers, and put the end of the gun in my mouth. I felt terrible; I wanted to throw up. I have never felt so bad in my life. I think I know exactly how she was feeling." It was very moving to watch him share the story with us. "I don't know how long we sat there, sharing whatever misery she was going through.

"After awhile my feelings cleared. I slowly pulled the gun out of my mouth just a few inches. After what seemed like forever, I sensed my sister do the same. I waited, and then moved the gun away from my face; again, after what seemed like an eternity, my sister copied me. I had tears running down my cheeks. I hadn't looked at her all this time, because we were sitting side by side, but I knew she must be crying, too." His eyes refocused and he looked pleased. "Eventually I put the gun on the floor in front of me; my sister did the same. I don't know why I did it, but I couldn't think of a thing to say to her. I only knew I had to do *something*."

I'm eternally grateful that he shared his story with us. It is a valuable illustration of how synchrony and body language can be more powerful than the spoken word.

Synchronize Voice Characteristics

As we've just seen, simply synchronizing body language makes a huge difference in being able to connect and convince. It sends a message: "I am with you. I'm on the same page now." Now take it a step further by synchronizing vocal characteristics. Synchronizing with another person's voice creates rapport unconsciously, not only in face-to-face situations but also in voice-only situations, such as on the telephone. Match the mood, energy, and pace of the other person. These vocal characteristics come from the speed, pitch, tone, and volume of the voice.

EXERCISE

Make Your Voice Match

For one day, have fun with matching the volume, speed, tone, and pitch (the ups and downs) of the people you meet. Don't go over the top. Do as little as you need to adjust to them.

Simply put, nothing drives a fast talker around the bend faster than a slow talker. Nothing unhinges a quiet talker more than the bellowing of a loud talker, and nothing grates on a smooth talker more than the braying of a whiny voice. I think you get the idea.

If you synchronize your body language, attitude, and tone of voice with another person, their feelings will rub off on you. You will begin to feel like them!

Convincing and Congruence

When your body language, tone of voice, and words are all saying the same thing, you have a complete attitude—it's called being *congruent.* What it really means is that you're believable. Let's turn on *The Tonight Show* again for a minute. If Leno came out one night and told the audience, "We're really going to have fun tonight!" while his body and his facial expressions looked genuinely angry, you wouldn't be convinced. Body language trumps both the tone of voice and the words we use.

Go up to someone you know and say, "I'm really having a great day," while shaking your head from side to side, as if to say no. See if they believe your words over your gestures. They won't. Now try saying the same thing with an angry voice. Will they believe you? Of course not. The tone of your voice conveys your true feelings.

In 1967, at the University of California at Los Angeles, Dr. Albert Mehrabian published a paper titled "Decoding of Inconsistent Communication." In it, he reported that in face-to-face communication, 55 percent of what we respond to takes place visually; 38 percent is the sound of the communication; and only 7 percent involves the actual words we use. In other words, people will first give credibility to what they see—to your gestures and body language—then to the tone of your voice, and last of all to the words you use. When the three *V*s—the visual, the vocal, and the verbal—are saying the same thing, we call that being congruent—or being convincing.

In face-to-face communication, people give most credibility to what they see, next to voice tone, and least to the words they're hearing.

I recently found myself sitting in the conference room of a national media corporation giving one-on-one accelerated training to several senior managers. Terry, the vice president of production, sat across the table from me. "I know all about the theory of creating rapport with people, but I can't make it stick," he said. Terry was quick to point out that he had lofty ambitions within the company but had been passed over for promotion several times. "People listen to me, but I can't build relationships." In these first few seconds, Terry's problem, or at least a large part of it, was written all over him.

He sat across from me with his elbows resting on the boardroom table and his hands steepled, like when you pray, his fingertips tapping against his lips as he spoke. His voice came out in jerks and starts as his eyes darted all over the place, looking for thoughts and words. Terry's body was indicating feelings of nervousness and impatience. My body picked up what his body was feeling and made me feel the same way. It turned out that he gave off these signals of impatience all the time. The result was that when other people sought Terry's opinion, they frequently began with phrases like, "This won't take but a moment," or "I won't keep you long."

But here's the real kicker: While other people thought Terry was impatient almost to the point of being rude, he thought he was giving off enthusiasm and energy.

Terry was incongruent; he was sending out mixed messages. His ability to connect with others and deliver his well-intentioned messages was jeopardized, along with his chances for promotion.

Fortunately, Terry's problem was easy to fix. First I showed him how to move his breathing from his chest to his belly: from his normal, anxious, fight-or-flight type breathing to the more relaxed and centered type practiced in the martial arts or by professional speakers and musicians. (You'll learn how to do this on pages 281–282.)

Second, we ran a tonality check. I chose four attitudes: *angry, surprised, worried,* and *gentle*. Then I showed him a list of four phrases: "We have to take action," "I'm hungry," "What happened at last week's briefing?" and, as the fourth, the day's date, "August 14."

I asked him to pick an attitude and say one of the phrases. My job was to figure out which attitude he had chosen. At first I was way off. When he thought he was sounding surprised, I thought he was angry; when he thought he was gentle, I thought he was worried.

If your words and body language aren't saying the same thing, people get confused and put off.

Next we reversed the roles. Interestingly enough, he was virtually spot on at picking up on me. He took the lead one more time, and I asked him to pause and close his eyes for a moment, pay attention to his breathing, and remember a time when he actually felt the feeling he was trying to express, and *then* say the phrase. Bingo! It worked. Terry's business personality had been getting in the way of his emotions. The more Terry calmed his breathing, the more his voice began to reflect his true feelings.

You will recall that in order to be convincing, you first have to be perceived as credible. When you are not congruent, people get suspicious because you don't look as if you mean what you say. Once Terry learned to be congruent, his relationship problem became a thing of the past.

Feedback—Give It, Get It

At the heart of Terry's problem was a disconnect in giving and getting feedback. Feedback from other people regulates and controls much more than the ebb and flow of face-to-face communication; it is responsible for our vital body rhythms, our emotional balance, our health, and our sanity. We cannot survive without feedback from other people.

Did you see the movie *Cast Away,* with Tom Hanks? The only way he survived psychologically and emotionally while he was alone on that desert island was to invent someone he could talk to and get feedback from. He made a volleyball into a person's head (called Wilson) and then projected a personality onto it. It became his best friend. He talked to it, shared his feelings with it, and asked it for advice. Tom and Wilson shared a deep emotional relationship. Wilson kept him sane. If you haven't seen the movie, this might sound a little crazy, but the fact is that without feedback from other people, our body rhythms become chaotic and we become ill at ease.

No one likes talking to a wall. Respond to people, and the connection you make will get stronger.

When you are making connections with other people, feedback is responsible for the ongoing quality of the encounter. Imagine playing tennis by yourself. If you bang the ball over the net and it doesn't come back, you'll have to bang another one over. And another. Pretty soon you'll get fed up.

People who don't give feedback appear boring and baffling, and their behavior becomes a self-fulfilling prophecy. Connecting is a two-way arrangement, in which the participants encourage each other along. If you look and act interested, I assume you are interested. If you don't react or respond, I assume you are not interested and I wish I was someplace else. Use your body and your face to show your interest. Lean forward, lean sideways, sit on the edge of your seat, smile, frown, shrug your shoulders, throw your hands in the air, nod, laugh, cry . . . *respond!* When your boss, or a client, or a colleague speaks with you, give feedback. A constant frustration I hear from employees is about bosses who don't give feedback.

Watch how others give feedback, especially people you admire. Look for counterproductive feedback—feedback that breaks the connection. Practice making your responses as subtle, and yet identifiable, as you can. Notice how people acknowledge feedback.

In my classes, I ask the participants to fill out a form and let me know when they have finished by using nonverbal feedback only—and to make sure I have received their message. You'd be amazed at the range of responses, from waving hands to winks, from adjusting eyeglasses to touching the nose, from big smiley nods to almost imperceptible narrowing of the eyes. As a general rule, the subtler you are, the more intimacy you achieve. At an auction, some folks bid by waving or making big gestures,

EXERCISE

Feedback

Today, play with feedback. When you are engaged in a conversation or attending a meeting, you can show you understand and agree or disagree by using body language only (nods, smiles, and so forth), spoken language only ("Yes," "No," "Sure," "How come?"), or both. Give feedback for a minute or two, and then withhold it. Give only nonverbal feedback. Give only spoken feedback. Give both. Give none. See how little feedback you can give; see how subtle you can be.

while the more seasoned bidders make almost imperceptible gestures. Subtlety radiates confidence.

Well-delivered feedback makes people feel that you are giving them your attention and that what they are communicating to you is having an impact.

In the broader picture, all of life is about feedback. All behavior is a feedback loop and a response to some kind of stimulus. You evolve and advance by knowing what you want, taking action, getting feedback, and using that feedback to change what you do until you get what you want. The better you are at processing feedback, the better the quality of your life.

As a rule, the subtler you are, the more intimacy you achieve.

When you connect with other people, be it in business or socially, your aim is to be welcomed into the other person's space, not excluded from it. By adjusting your attitude, opening your heart, synchronizing body language, being congruent, and giving and responding to feedback, you will set the other person's natural instincts for survival at ease.

90-Second Summary

Attitude Is Key

- Attitude is infectious. It's the first thing about you that people notice, and it immediately rubs off on those around you.

- Attitude is made up of your body language, your tone of voice, and your choice of words. If you are enthusiastic, then look enthusiastic, sound enthusiastic, and use enthusiastic words.

- You can control and adjust your attitude *if you want to.* Your mind and your body are one system—change one and the other will follow.

- Learn to distinguish between attitudes that are really useful and attract people to us (being warm, enthusiastic, and confident) and attitudes that are really useless and repel people (being angry, arrogant, or impatient).

Body Language

Become conscious of what your body language says, because it accounts for more than half of what others respond to when connecting with you.

- Open body language—uncrossed legs and arms, good eye contact, smiling, leaning forward—exposes the heart and is welcoming. It signals, "I'm open for business."
- Closed body language—arms crossed defensively, avoiding eye contact, hiding your hands, moving away—defends the heart and repels. It signals, "I'm closed for business."
- Pointing your heart—not obstructed by folded arms, clipboards, or bundles of papers—at the heart of those you meet is an easy way to demonstrate you are open for business.

Synchronizing Body Language and Voice Characteristics

People in rapport unconsciously synchronize each other's body language and vocal characteristics. If you deliberately synchronize your body with another's, you will create a sense of understanding and trust and amazing connections can happen. Likewise, if you synchronize your voice—speak slowly to a slow talker, animatedly to a quick talker, quietly to a quiet talker—you will quickly develop a sense of rapport.

Congruence

When your body language, tone of voice, and words are all saying the same thing, you are congruent, or believable. In order to be persuasive, you must first be credible. If your words and your body language aren't saying the same thing, people will be confused and put off. So make sure that your body isn't giving off signals—whether it's impatience, irritation, or inattention—that your words are not.

Feedback

- Give and respond to feedback, both verbal and nonverbal: Look and act interested, lean forward, sit on the edge of your seat, smile, shrug your shoulders, laugh. If you don't react or respond, people will assume you're not interested and wish they were someplace else.
- Feedback gives design, direction, and depth to encounters. While you are making connections, feedback is responsible for the ongoing quality of the encounter.
- Well-delivered feedback makes people feel that you are giving them your attention and that what they are communicating to you is having an impact.

4 Speak the Language of the Brain

When it comes to making an immediate connection, good intentions can take us places we never meant to go. Listen to this airline pilot I recently flew with: "Howdy folks, this is the captain. It's good to have you aboard. Now that we're on our way, I thought I'd just take a few moments to let you know that we don't anticipate any bad weather, so we shouldn't encounter any bumps, and if everything goes according to plan, there shouldn't be any problem arriving on time in London."

Yikes! All of a sudden every bit of high-flying anxiety I ever felt had been activated. I'd had one of those good-karma days—smooth sailing on the way to the airport, polite check-in staff, a great seat. But now, here was the captain reciting every frequent flier's worst fears—a rough ride, bad weather, and problems arriving on time at the other end. And I wasn't the only one to feel this way. There were plenty of nervous glances exchanged between the other passengers.

Our pilot had failed to connect with his passengers because he didn't talk in the positive and say what he wanted to say, which was, "Sit back and relax, it's going to be a smooth flight, and we'll be arriving on time." Which is exactly how it turned out. By failing to talk in the positive, the pilot planted a host of negative suggestions in the passengers' heads.

Your Brain Can Process Only Positive Information

Where's the milk in your refrigerator? I'm sure you know, but how do you know? Here's how: You made a lightning-fast picture in your mind's eye of the inside of your refrigerator and saw where the milk was. Amazing.

What's your favorite Rolling Stones song (or any band you really love)? Got it? How did you do that? You played it back in your head to check it out.

What does sand feel like? Same concept. You went inside your head to retrieve sensory information, to check out your experience.

This is the language of the brain—pictures, sounds, and feelings. Spoken language comes after input from the senses. Now, can you make a picture of yourself not doing something? Not feeling something? Not seeing something? You can't, because the brain can't process negative pictures, sounds, or feelings. Here's what I mean. In your mind's eye, can you make a picture of yourself *not* feeding a dog? No, you can't. All you can do is make a picture of yourself doing something else—standing by the dog, walking the dog, bungee jumping with the dog. These are all pictures of you not feeding a dog. Your brain can work only with positive information. It gets this information from the experiences of your five senses, which it then manipulates in the emotional blender we call the imagination.

More Pleasure, or More Problems?

I recently purchased a new computer system for my office. When I thanked the woman for her help, she replied, "No problem."

Problem? Where did a problem suddenly come from? I never thought of problems—until now. Let's try again.

"Thanks for your help today."

"It was a pleasure."

Ah, "pleasure." Now that feels much better. Give me pleasure over problems any day, even subconsciously—and subconsciously is how much of our language processing goes on. Do you prefer to be greeted with "How goes the battle?" or "Good to see you"?

Become aware of the embedded messages in the words you choose. Say "My pleasure," or "You're welcome," instead of "No problem."

Let's start at the simplest possible level. If you teach a dog to jump up when you say "Jump up," what do you think the dog will do when you say "Don't jump up" without changing the tone of your voice?

That's right—the dog will jump up! Even when we humans, who can process language, hear you say, "Don't jump up," we first have to think about jumping up, and then do something else instead. This is because "don't," and all negation, really isn't language.

So, if "don't," or negation generally, doesn't register with the brain, then what should I expect my daughter's first thought to be when I say "Please don't mess up your room"?

Recently, I gave a keynote speech at a resort where the swimming pool curved its way in and out of the convention hall. As part of the welcoming speech, the president of the association joked with the attendees, "Please don't fall into the pool." You could see their eyes glaze over momentarily as they pictured themselves doing just that. We even do this to ourselves when we say things like "I don't want to mess up this deal." And how many of us have ended a letter with the line "If you want more information, please don't hesitate to contact me"?

How many negative suggestions do you plant in the minds of your customers, clients, colleagues, patients, or students with the words you choose and use every day? Sure, you can make a case semantically for saying that as long as your customers and clients know what you mean, it's okay. But bearing in mind that the brain has to first think of a behavior and then think of the opposite behavior to replace it, what thoughts are you really awakening in your clients, superiors, or staff when you say the following? Can you spot the positive and negative messages here?

- Don't worry about the dip in the market.
- No problem.
- Invest for the long term.
- Don't panic!
- We won't do anything reckless.
- Call me when you want more information.
- I wouldn't take him too seriously.
- We've covered all the bases.
- This won't hurt a bit.
- There's no way you can lose.
- It was a pleasure.

This is where the *K* (*know* what you want—in the positive) in your *KFC* kicks in yet again. In business, you must be aware of how you use language and you must encourage your staff to be aware, too, and to get into the habit of thinking and speaking in the positive. Or to put it another way: Learn not to speak in the negative. (Process that!)

Mood over Matter

As the human brain processes the information and experiences fed into it by the five senses, the sensations are transformed into language. On a certain level, there are, in fact, only six things we do on a day-to-day basis. Five of these six have to do with our senses: We see, hear, touch, taste, and smell. What do you think the only other thing is? We process language: We process our experiences into words and communicate them.

Every day we go out into the world and have experiences through our senses. Then we explain our experiences, first to ourselves and then to others. We think in words (we talk to ourselves) and then we talk to the world, explaining our experiences.

We spend a tremendous part of our lives explaining our experiences. It's one of the key components in connecting with other people. Explaining is hard work, and one problem that almost all of us have is that we fall into patterns of explaining our experiences in preordained ways. What's more, sooner or later we think without thinking!

Everyone has an explanatory style. Some people develop the habit of explaining their experiences to themselves and others in a positive way, while others do most of their explaining from a negative point of view. There are many shades of explanatory style, but primarily they break down into positive and negative.

A positive explanatory style results in your being perceived as enthusiastic, optimistic, and very good at spotting opportunities. A negative style can get you tagged as anything from a realist who's good at spotting problems to an outright pessimist. These styles affect your attitude, and as you well know by now, attitude is infectious.

I'm sure our pilot, if he gave it any thought, felt he was being practical and realistic with his announcement, but his explanatory style influenced his choice of words and, in turn, the outcome of his communication. The good news is that you can choose your style of explaining, and hence further shape your attitude. And when you accomplish that, you can shape how you make other people feel and how they feel about you.

It all comes down to this: As your experiences become words, your words become actions, your actions become habits, your habits become character, and your character becomes your destiny.

Cause and Effect

We all have an innate urge to explain why things happen. The best tools we have for this are cause-and-effect statements. There are two ways to make such statements. One is to attribute the cause to something outside of you: "That idiot in accounting put me in a bad mood." The other way is to attribute it to something inside you: "I'm a genius!"

Of course, neither one of these attributions is always correct, but the key to finding out which one is right often lies in the use of one simple word—a word that is one of the greatest connectors there is. That word is "why."

Kids know this. They're great interviewers. As far as I can tell, they're preprogrammed to ask "Why?" "Why are we going in here?" "Why is he wearing that thing in his nose?" "Why are you driving so fast?" It's innate, natural curiosity. And sooner or later, that innate curiosity gets squelched, minimized just like a computer window, by adults who've almost been driven mad by the incessant "Why? Why? Why?" of their kids. But it's always there inside us, operating in the background, even when we're adults and think that it's gone.

We evolve as a species through logic, reasoning, comparing, and, most important, processing feedback. Curiosity—the instinct that goes with "why"—is a critical element in this process. Have you ever noticed that your brain finds it much more satisfying to process information in a cause-and-effect situation than in a cause-only, or effect-only situation? That's because . . .

There you are. I could have finished my previous comments before the word "because." However, when I introduced the word "because," it seemed to lead to something much more satisfying, to the logical fulfillment of your natural curiosity, and it was offering the prospect of a complete explication of cause and effect. In other words: When you do this, that happens. How can we use this to our advantage when connecting in business (or anywhere, for that matter)?

You increase your chances for compliance if you offer a reason why you want something done.

"Because . . ."

Telling people the reason why you are doing something has a major influence on how they react to you because, more often than not, people willingly comply with requests when given reasons why they should. Ellen Langer, a social psychologist at Harvard University, demonstrated this in a study that set out to show that people respond automatically and without thinking when given the proper stimulus. And that stimulus was a resolution of cause and effect.

Here's how it went: In a busy library, one of her subjects would approach the person at the front of the line for the photocopier and say, "Excuse me, I have five pages. May I use the Xerox machine because I am in a rush?" This request was convincing 94 percent of the time. Later, when the subject returned to ask another group of people lined up at the same machine and said, "Excuse me, I have five pages. May I use the Xerox machine?" her success rate dropped to 60 percent. No big surprise here. What *was* a big surprise was that when the subject approached the front of the line a little later and asked, "Excuse me, I have five pages. May I use the Xerox machine because I have to make these copies?" the compliance rate whizzed back up to 93 percent!

Automatic response is based on reason, or at least the appearance of reason. People need to have reasons to make decisions and justify their actions. Langer's experiment showed that even when the reason is not really a reason, but only *looks* like a reason, it's enough to trigger a positive response. Because the word "because" is usually followed by information and has become, for most people, a trigger, it is powerful enough to set in motion a patterned response—in this case a "yes" response, even in the absence of concrete information. This is the same as a handshake. When someone extends their right hand toward you, you do the same without thinking. When you want to connect quickly, offer your contact a "because" and chances are you'll be successful. For example, if you're aiming to do business with company Q, and you meet a key contact there, instead of simply saying, "I'm delighted to meet you," add "because I've read so much about your pioneering work with XYZ. . . ."

90-Second Summary

Your Brain Can Process Only Positive Information

The language of the brain is pictures, sounds, feelings, and, to a lesser extent, smells and tastes. The brain can't process negative pictures (*not* doing something, *not* seeing something); it can work only with positive information. So be conscious not to plant negative suggestions in others' minds with the words you choose. (How's that for a double negative!)

- Speak in the positive.
- Say "It's a pleasure" instead of "No problem."

- Use the words "Call me" instead of "Don't hesitate to call."

Explanatory Style

When explaining our experiences to ourselves and others, we tend to fall into patterns. Consciously develop a positive explanatory style, and infect others with your upbeat attitude.

Cause and Effect

Telling people the reason why you are doing something has a major influence on how they react to you. People tend to automatically comply with requests when given a reason why they should. Keep reading because you'll learn a lot.

5
Connect with the Senses

Carl Jung observed that his patients had different ways of communicating their experiences—some of them expressed themselves in pictures, others talked about how things sounded to them, and others spoke about how things felt.

In the mid-seventies, I was flown to Miami to be briefed for a cruise-line photo shoot for a new advertising campaign. The agency team told me, "We know that everyone wants good food and fresh air when they go on vacation; that's a given. But our research also tells us that people have sensory preferences. Some folks choose a vacation primarily for beautiful scenery; others to get away to somewhere comfortable, with activities; and yet others are primarily searching for peace and quiet. We know that all three aspects are critical to the decision-making process, but the final choice comes from satisfying the person's sensory preference." I was told that my photos had to appeal to all three groups: the seeing people, the feeling people, and the hearing people.

Dr. Jung would have been proud. What the cruise line's ad agency knew about connecting is true for us all—different people choose to take in the world through different senses. And if we want to convince them, we have to figure out which sense they favor.

Sensory Preferences

By the time we reach our teens, we have come to favor one of the three main senses—sight, sound, or touch—in the way we interpret the world. Of course, we use all of our senses, but some people rely more on the visual, others on the auditory, and yet others on the kinesthetic (touch, or physical sensation). Inevitably, our dominant sense becomes the one we primarily use to communicate with ourselves and others. Some researchers estimate that 55 percent of people are visual, 30 percent are kinesthetic, and 15 percent auditory. Others see the split as 40 percent, 40 percent, and 20 percent, respectively.

Obviously, the most effective way to communicate is by adapting your communication style to the person you're communicating with. By that I mean, if they think in pictures, talk to them in pictures, or at least talk about how things look. If they favor sounds, tell them how things sound, and if they are concerned with physical sensation, tell them how things feel.

If you want to motivate or convince, ground your message in pictures, physical sensation, or sound.

Let's say I'm a travel agent and someone comes into my agency and says, "I want to go on vacation." If I can immediately figure out that the person is, let's say, kinesthetic, I'd say, "How would you feel about a place where the sand is soft, the water's warm, and the beds are comfortable?" In other words, I'd tell them how it *feels* because that's how they make their decisions (subconsciously, of course).

If I figured out they were auditory, I'd say, "How does this sound to you? I know of a place where all you can hear is the waves and the gulls, and it's away from all the hullabaloo of the city." And if they were visual, I'd show them the pictures. "Just look at this."

But—you're probably asking—how can you know which way to pitch them the moment they walk in the door? Here are some of the clues I'd be looking for from the very outset of our encounter.

Visual people talk about the way things look. They tend to speak with high, fast, straight-to-the-point voices because they can't understand why you don't immediately see what they see. They want to *see* proof of your assertions before they make decisions. Their breathing will be high in the chest and rapid. Visuals dress to impress and often exhibit upright posture. Visuals want eye contact when they speak. They are offended by untidiness, mess, and clutter.

Visuals consistently refer to the look of things: "Now that we've seen the possibilities, we can look toward the future." "From my point of view, it looks like our goal is in sight now. Do you see what I mean?" As a general rule, people look up to the left or right when looking for a picture. (When I ask you what color your favorite shirt is, where do your eyes go?) Their gestures are up and out, sometimes drawing pictures in the air.

Auditory people talk about the way things sound. They usually have a way with words and they can be very persuasive, with smooth and engaging voices. They tend toward adventurous thinking. They talk a little more slowly than visuals, breathing steadily from low in the chest.

An auditory person will often be the one that makes a tasteful statement with the way he or she dresses. An auditory person may turn her head slightly to one side when listening. She's actually turning her ear toward you and defocusing her eyes so as to concentrate on the sound of what you're saying. Auditory people are turned off by unpleasant sounds, noises, and voices.

When you hear someone who is constantly referencing

the sound of things—"I didn't like his tone of voice," "What he said had a familiar ring to it," "I'm only voicing my opinion," "She had me completely tongue-tied," "She told a terrific story and received a thunderous applause"—you've probably found an auditory person.

As a general rule, auditory people look to the sides (toward their ears, in essence) when looking for a sound. (Where do your eyes go when I ask you whether the national anthem sounds better sung by an adult or by a child?) Auditories frequently look to the side when talking, and will break eye contact to concentrate on recovering a sound from their mental files. Gestures will often match the rhythm of their words, and they sometimes touch their mouth, jaw, or ears as they talk.

Kinesthetic people talk about the way things feel. They tend to be sentimental, easygoing, and intuitive, though sometimes they are reserved and cautious. If you're dealing with someone who is either full-figured or extremely athletic, you may well be dealing with a kinesthetic person. Kinesthetics can be fairly easy to identify because they are hands-on people who gain satisfaction from touching and feeling. Their wardrobes tend to be comfortable and full of interesting textures, and to put functionality ahead of fashion.

Some . . . kinesthetic . . . people . . . have . . . been . . . known . . . to talk . . . agonizingly . . . slowly, or to throw in all sorts of details that make the visuals and auditories want to scream, "I got it ten minutes ago!" They have deeper, slower voices than the rest. Kinesthetics tend to be detail oriented.

Kinesthetic folk favor physical, touchy-feely language: "I'm leaning heavily toward giving it a shot." "We have a few stumbling blocks, but we'll straighten it all out." "I'll try to iron out any confusion." "When I can put my finger on something concrete, I'll get in touch with her and walk her through it." "Let's all stay cool, calm, and collected." When accessing feelings or coding, storing, or retrieving information, they generally look down and to their right. Breathing is regular and from low in the belly. Gestures are low, arms or hands frequently folded on the chest or abdomen.

If you can figure out what sense a person favors, you can speak in terms he or she will immediately connect with—and you'll both benefit.

Needless to say, if you can figure out just which sensory type you're dealing with, you're well on your way to connecting with them. Because if you can speak in terms that mean the most to them, your message will immediately make sense to them.

Eye Cues

The eyes can give even more valuable clues about how a person thinks. As mentioned above, visual people will tend to look up more, while auditories spend more time looking sideways, and kinesthetics look down. This is because they each favor one sense to code and store general information as well as express it. If you asked, "How was the Stones concert?" a visual would first remember how it looked, an auditory how it sounded, and a kinesthetic how it felt. But eye cues can tell you more than who you're dealing with; they can also tell you *what* you're dealing with. When people look up, or sideways to their right, they are probably constructing, or coming up with, their answer. When they look up, or sideways to their left, they are more than likely remembering it.

Rapport by Design— The Heart of the Chameleon

Rapport is mutual trust and understanding between two or more people. It's not a big surprise to discover that visuals look pretty good to visuals, auditories sound all right to auditories, and kinesthetics find themselves leaning toward kinesthetics. There are always some people we find rapport with naturally and become friends

EXERCISE

Sensory Language

On the left you'll find a description of a person; on the right you'll find some phrases. First determine which person is visual, which is auditory, and which is kinesthetic, and then see if you can match them up with the phrases.

Jill runs a successful catering company. She started out on her own and now employs forty-three people. A pastry chef by training, she still enjoys rolling up her sleeves and giving a hand wherever she's needed. She prefers comfortable clothes and has a patient, kind voice.

We all have differing viewpoints.

Can you grasp the basics?

That sounds like a great idea.

Show me how you did it.

I hear you loud and clear.

with—because we share the same tastes and interests, and probably the same sensory preferences. We call this *rapport by chance.* But in business we can't leave *rapport to chance.* We can't simply assume or hope that we'll be dealing with people like ourselves. We know from experience that it doesn't work that way. So, for everyone else, there is *rapport by design.*

Howard is a no-nonsense lawyer. He deals in facts and wants to see the evidence. He's a snappy dresser and likes to look people in the eye when he talks to them. He expects the same in return.

Melissa can charm the birds out of the trees: She has a wonderful way with words. She has been in politics since her early twenties and has lots of friends. Her dress style is flexible and always seems to match the tone of the occasion.

I see what you're saying.

We're up against the wall.

Can you shed some light on this problem?

That name rings a bell.

I can't put my finger on anything concrete.

Are you tuning in to what she's saying?

Let's explore a little deeper.

To check your answers, see page 111.

If we make our best efforts to create mutual trust and understanding—by adjusting our attitude and by synchronizing our body language, voice characteristics, preferred words, and sensory preferences with those we work with—we will find rapport with them, and making deals, achieving mutual goals, and initiating projects will all be much easier.

90-Second Summary

Sensory Preferences

The most effective way to transfer information from you to someone else is to adapt your communication style to match his or hers. People generally fall into one of three categories:

- **Visual.** Tell or show me how it looks. Visual people need to see pictures and make images of their experiences.
- **Auditory.** Tell or show me how it sounds. Auditory people need to hear sounds and verbalize their experiences.
- **Kinesthetic.** Tell or show me how it feels. Kinesthetic people communicate by expressing physical sensation.

Rapport by Design

Establish rapport with others by synchronizing your body language, voice characteristics, preferred words, and sensory preferences with theirs.

Sensory Language Exercise Answers:

Jill is kinesthetic, Howard is visual, and Melissa is auditory.

Jill would likely say, “Can you grasp the basics?” “We’re up against the wall.” “I can’t put my finger on anything concrete.” “Let’s explore a little deeper.”

Howard would likely say, “We all have differing viewpoints.” “Show me how you did it.” “I see what you’re saying.” “Can you shed some light on this problem?”

Melissa would likely say, “That sounds like a great idea.” “I hear you loud and clear.” “That name rings a bell.” “Are you tuning in to what she’s saying?”

Part Three

Connecting with Personality

Once you have connected with a person's basic human instincts and they feel comfortable enough to trust you, you enter the second phase: connecting your world with theirs. To achieve this, you need to know three things: how personalities connect and react, the true nature of your business and the role you play in it, and how to package yourself in a way that best manifests your personality and your capabilities to the external world, where you contribute and make a living.

Business is about getting ideas across to others, from one personality to another. Learning how to identify and motivate the various personality types (including your own) will enable you to deliver your message in the most effective way possible.

Strange but true, money is not the cause of success in business (though it is one of the effects). I'll show you how to pinpoint what motivates you, and link it to your work so you can succinctly articulate what you do, see clearly where your path lies, and stay merrily on track to inevitable success.

Packaging your personality to reflect the right blend of authority and approachability influences the quantity and quality of attention you get from others. Here you'll find out how to feel good and gain a competitive edge.

6 Feed the Personality

All business is about taking good ideas to market. You take a good idea, turn it into a big idea, and take it to the people.

In 1762, John Montagu, the Earl of Sandwich, had a good idea. He was a big-time gambler who didn't like to leave the gaming table. When he became hungry, he told his servants, "Bring me a slice of meat between two slices of bread." This was the birth of the sandwich.

Henry Heinz had a good idea: He put tomato ketchup in a bottle. Levi Strauss had a good idea: He made trousers out of tent cloth. Bill Gates had a good idea: to put a computer on every desk. John Kimberly and Charles Clark had a good idea: a soft tissue paper to remove cold cream. Today you can eat a cheese sandwich while you boot up Windows in your Levi's and wipe the ketchup off your fingers with a Kleenex. These good ideas are now enduring big ideas, and have created jobs for countless thousands of us and built considerable fortunes for their originators. And it all happened thanks to an army of doers who backed up the original dreamers.

Dreamers and Doers

There are four processes that constitute the core business model: dreaming, analyzing, persuading, and controlling. Accordingly there are four types of personality that businesses are always on the lookout for: dreamers, to come up with ideas; analyzers, to make sure the ideas will work; persuaders, to get the ideas appreciated; and controllers, to make sure things get done. Many successful entrepreneurs embody some or all of these qualities, while others find it necessary to find a partner to complete the equation.

Your personality affects both your job choice and your perceived job performance. Given a choice, people will usually choose jobs that fit their personality—an outgoing, sociable person (persuader) will be more likely to succeed in sales, whereas a more process-oriented, cautious type (analyst) may be more likely to excel in engineering. Someone who is assertive and outspoken by nature (controller) will be adept at managing others, while a person who is less assertive but able to see things from many angles (dreamer) will be more suited to a creative career.

Analysts and controllers feel more at home following logical procedures or guidelines, whereas dreamers and persuaders rely on emotional spontaneity and options to function at their best. Analysts and dreamers tend to be more reserved and introspective, whereas controllers and persuaders are more often than not outoging and assertive.

The Four Business Personalities

Procedures

Reserved			**Outgoing**
	Analyst	**Controller**	
	Dreamer	**Persuader**	

Options

How can you tell who's who? **A dreamer** is a visionary who plucks options and ideas out of the air and gives them focus. He does not give up easily—he tries and tries again. Connect with him at work by giving him room to dream, and respect his personal space.

An analyst's strengths come from being detail-oriented and a critical thinker. She is a precise problem solver with a strong drive to get the job done right. To connect with her at work, pay attention to detail, be well organized, and stick to the facts.

A persuader draws his strengths from outgoing optimism and by being an entertaining, persuasive communicator. He longs for appreciation. To connect with him at work, make him the center of attention, respond to him with enthusiasm, and appreciate his spontaneity. Put details down on paper, or chances are he'll lose his way.

A controller is fearlessly competitive, results-oriented, direct, and self-confident. She's driven by an overriding desire to get the job done. To connect with her at work, give her options and alternatives. Bury what you want among the options and focus on it. Let her know that you understand and appreciate what she does best, and above all don't waste her time.

There's a downside to each of these types as well. A dreamer without dreams can become a flake. An analyst without a meaty project can easily turn into a complainer. A persuader who can't persuade becomes a bore. A controller who can't control anymore can become a despot. To be effective, each of these types must be aware not only of their strengths but of their weaknesses as well. When they are—and can find a partner who can make up for their weaknesses or shortcomings—great things can ensue. For example, let's look at a great pair—an analyst/controller named Rachel and a dreamer/persuader named Sam who together made one of Sam's dreams come true.

A few years back, Sam and Rachel were walking along their town's seafront, and Sam saw a FOR RENT sign in a store window.

"Do you know what this place needs? A really good seafood restaurant," Sam said to Rachel.

"You're right," Rachel agreed, and her mind started whirring. She thought about other restaurants in the area. Would there be enough business in the off-season? How reliable were the local suppliers? After she laid to rest the perceived obstacles, she prepared a business plan, and together they went to the local bank manager to persuade him to lend them $45,000.

Sam did most of the talking, and the bank manager was convinced—with one proviso. He looked straight at Rachel and said, "I'll go for it as long as you control the business."

Sam had come up with the original idea and had done a good job of convincing the bank manager. But the manager had listened closely every time Rachel described her analysis of their restaurant's potential and its potential challenges. It didn't take him long to figure out who would make the better controller.

Rachel was organized, detail-oriented, and realistic (like him)—and he liked how, in the nicest possible way, she curbed Sam's natural impetuosity. As long as Sam and Rachel understood their roles, the business would likely be a success. But force Rachel into the creative end or make Sam an analyst, and the bank will have to whistle for its money.

Just as it's important to understand the personalities of your staff, colleagues, and bosses, it's important that you know yourself. Your personality shapes the way you frame and present your ideas to others, so first you need to understand who you are and how you connect. Take a look at this controller, who managed to get into the heads of a bunch of dreamers and figured out how to help them get the job done.

Steve Erickson owns a packaging/design company. His creative staff seems to have a collective block—the work that's been coming out of the department for the last month has been subpar. He knows that he's been putting a lot of pressure on them, but he has a hard time understanding why that should make a difference.

"Everybody's under pressure lately," he told me. "My instinct is to get tough with them, to tell them that their work has been subpar, to tell them they're being paid to do great work and nothing but. A few years ago, I'd have just pulled them into the conference room and told them,

'Here's what I need from you over the next quarter, and it had better be good or you're gone.'" But Steve had already learned that this approach wouldn't cut it.

I met Steve at one of my seminars when his hand went up during a discussion of dreamers. He'd asked some very perceptive questions, and at the end of the day we got together for a few minutes and chatted about how to motivate his creative crew.

"Your staff are professional dreamers, and you are a controller," I told him. I didn't tell him specifically how to deal with them, but I did tell him how to engage a dreamer's imagination. I explained that the way things look, sound, feel, and even smell and taste is essential to his team's productivity and that a constant flow of new experiences and stimuli is essential to their process. He admitted that the current stimuli obviously weren't working. Although his instinct was to get tough with them, he realized that it would be completely counterproductive to pressure them. Instead, he decided to work his *KFC*—figure out what he wanted, in the positive, and find a way to get it.

I heard from Steve later that he caused a bit of an uproar at his company when he decided to take his team off-site for a retreat to try to jump-start their creativity. Some of his executive team thought he was rewarding this team for not performing.

"Take them to a five-star hotel when they haven't given us what we need? You must be nuts," the VP of finance had told him. But that's exactly what Steve did, and what he got was exactly what the company needed.

Steve's short-term solution was to take the department away for a weekend workshop at a great old luxury hotel in the Adirondack Mountains. Once everyone was away from the office and in touch with the right kinds of stimuli, they got more done on their most pressing project that weekend than they had in the previous month. And the energy they created went back to the office with them. Steve's medium-term solution was to redecorate their offices with bright red swinging saloon doors and a matching red carpet, and to plant a fifteen-foot tree outside the window. If they'd been a bunch of analysts, this would not have been the right move, but for Steve's dreamers it worked wonders.

When Personalities Collide

Look around your office. Is there someone you don't get along with particularly well? What personality type is he or she? What type are you? If you can figure this out, you may be able to break the impasse. When two people don't know why they're at odds or don't understand who they're dealing with, the breakdown in communication can be quick and enduring.

Do you have a colleague with whom you don't get along? What personality type are you? What type is he? Knowing this may help you break the impasse.

John Stevenson is a regional sales manager for Acme Corp. He's having his first meeting with the new regional head of sales from the district west of his. He found out that they were both going to be passing through O'Hare Airport at the same time and arranged for them to meet during their layovers. John wants to compare notes and go over the new order forms he had a hand in developing.

John is a member of the airline's executive club, and as his flight was scheduled to arrive forty minutes ahead of Sandy's, he arranged to meet her there. He is a sensible man who wears sensible clothes.

"John Stevenson?" He looked up from the copy of *Fortune* he'd been studying to see an energetic, grinning woman in a canary yellow suit standing in front of him, juggling two shoulder bags and a briefcase, in case she had to shake hands.

"Sandy?"

"Yes." She nodded vigorously.

"Please sit down. I thought you said you weren't a member. I was going to—"

"Oh, I'm not, but I talked my way in, and they showed me where you were sitting, at least they thought it was you. They were pretty sure, so I said I'd just go over and check, and if it wasn't you, I'd just come back and wait. They're pretty busy out there. And so here we are." She had managed to arrange her bags and sit down without missing a beat.

Yes, indeed. Would you like a refreshment?" When she

EXERCISE

Who's Talking?

The business chameleon must be able to adapt to and feed the personality types of her customers and colleagues. To do this, she must first figure out what type they are by observing, asking questions, and listening. Is she dealing with a dreamer, an analyzer, a persuader, or a controller? Once she makes the determination, then she immediately synchronizes her style with theirs.

Here are four different answers to the same question. Figure out who is the dreamer, the analyst, the persuader, and the controller. Try to imagine what you'd say next to connect with each of them and keep the conversation moving.

Question: How can we cut the skyrocketing cost in the design department?

said yes, John walked over to the snack bar and came back with a soft drink.

"We don't have long," he said, checking his watch. "About twenty-two minutes, to be precise, so if it's all right with you, I'd like to show you something."

Sandy was not prepared for such a quick start. John took two printed sheets from a neat pile he had organized on the table before she arrived and thrust them into her

Answer 1: Maybe we could run an independent publicity campaign pointing out the skyrocketing cost of overruns.

Answer 2: Move someone over from accounting with a ninety-day deadline to show measurable results.

Answer 3: Let's find out how many other departments have the same problems. If we look at the figures, maybe there's something design could learn from production or corporate communications.

Answer 4: With all the computers and wireless Internet connections, maybe we could design an early warning system that would pop up on our screens.

I'm sure you worked out that the questions were answered in order by a persuader, a controller, an analyst, and finally a dreamer.

hand. Sandy wanted to chat, but instead she sat there nodding at the sheets. She was normally good-natured, but this guy was beginning to tick her off.

"Slow down a second. What am I supposed to be looking at? What am I supposed to be looking for?"

"I put it all in an e-mail to you," John said, his exasperation showing both on his face and in his voice.

Time elapsed so far? Less than ninety seconds, and this relationship is already a nonstarter. Have you figured out where to place these two on the personality chart? What are their strengths, and the weaknesses in these strengths? What drives Sandy? What drives John?

This is a classic missed opportunity. John is an analyzer—precise and focused. Sandy is a persuader—wrapped up in herself and talking too much. John could have gotten a great conversation going by expressing his appreciation of Sandy's resourcefulness in finding him and thereby synchronized her air of freedom. Sandy could have complimented John on bringing them together here and synchronized his sense of organization. But as it is, a possible moment of cooperation and team building has been missed. In fact, they'll both remember this meeting and it will probably remain a slightly embarrassing moment that may keep them from ever developing a strong relationship.

Room for Improvement

One key to improving your communication skills is to look at the flip side of your strengths. I'm not saying that you should look at your weaknesses—quite the contrary. Look at the weaknesses inherent in your strengths. It's usually not your weaknesses that inhibit your ability to connect, convince, and have fun with all those around you, but the weaknesses in your strengths. For example, do any of the following apply to you?

Dreamers: Does your ability to see situations from many angles make you indecisive? Or could your need for personal space or lack of concern with personal appearance give others the wrong first impression? Do you sometimes say yes when you really mean no?

Analysts: Is your perfectionism making you miss out on the big-picture opportunities that come your way? Are you overly critical? Is it possible you push away others by appearing aloof or distant?

Persuaders: Are you so intent on being entertaining that you are prone to exaggerate? Do you talk so much that it drowns out useful feedback? Do you avoid confrontation? Do you have difficulty staying focused?

Controllers: Are you so self-assured that you're becoming a poor listener? Does your impatience make you argumentative or just plain stubborn? Could that tendency toward impatience be diminishing your ability to process feedback and make the connections you need?

Inherent in every strength is a weakness.

Sometimes what builds us up also drags us down. No one's perfect, of course, but an increased awareness of those aspects of yourself that need work is the first step toward improvement. So while you're building on your strengths, take time out to recognize the flip side of them and their impact on those around you. Also bear in mind that whatever your personality type, it is transmitting a tremendous amount of information to others. Be aware of what you're sending.

Controllers: Do you look aggressive or intimidating to people?

Analysts: Are you letting yourself appear standoffish or superior?

Persuaders: Do your many flamboyant gestures seem to confuse people?

Dreamers: Do people wonder if you're paying attention to them?

Even if you're dealing with a customer, client, or colleague you've known for years, once you understand their personality type, it will make a difference next time you connect.

90-Second Summary

The business chameleon adapts to and feeds the personality types of his customers and colleagues.

Personality Types

There are four basic personalities that businesses are always on the lookout for: dreamers, to come up with ideas; analyzers, to make sure the ideas will work; persuaders, to get the ideas appreciated; and controllers, to make sure things get done. Most people have a combination of these talents, but one usually dominates. Here's how to connect:

- **Dreamer.** Give her room and stimulus to dream. Respect her personal space. Talk in options.
- **Analyst.** Pay attention to detail, be well organized, and stick to the facts.
- **Persuader.** Respond to him with enthusiasm and appreciate his spontaneity. Put details down on paper.
- **Controller.** Give her options and alternatives (then try to steer her toward the outcome you want). Acknowledge her qualities and don't waste her time.

The Weaknesses in Your Strength

Examine the weaknesses inherent in your strengths to improve your communication skills.

- **Dreamer.** Are you indecisive? Do you give others the wrong first impression? Do you say yes when you really mean no? Or no when you really mean yes?
- **Analyst.** Do you miss out on big-picture opportunities? Are you overly critical? Do you appear aloof or distant?
- **Persuader.** Do you exaggerate or talk too much? Do you avoid confrontation? Do you have difficulty staying focused?
- **Controller.** Are you argumentative or stubborn? How well do you process feedback?

7

Know the Nature of Your Business

Despite what you may have been taught, money isn't the strongest motivator that you can offer a person. Sure, we all need the necessities of life that money can buy—food, shelter, transportation, and security—but what drives most people to go beyond the call of duty at the office is the chance to do work they believe is important. Doing work that feels important—to the company, to the bottom line, to your team, or to your community—makes your beliefs and values actually come alive. This allows you to experience a sense of worth, of usefulness, and of purpose and makes your ability to convince others second nature.

Smart companies recognize the value of tapping into their employees' values, of making their work meaningful. One of the ways they do this is by creating a mission statement. Some go even further and distill their mission statements down to what I call the company's big idea.

A carefully crafted *big-idea* statement can simply and memorably explain why the organization exists, and what difference it makes. It can give an organization a personality. The measure of the statement's effectiveness comes when every employee is able to reference it and instantly ask and answer the question "Am I doing it now, or not?"

For example, Marriott Hotels' big idea is, "We make people away from home feel as if they're among friends." It's brilliant, and easy to remember. Anyone from the head of public relations to the clerk at the front desk to the housekeeper in the rooms to the pastry chef in the kitchen can ask himself or herself, "Am I doing it now, or not?" If the answer is yes, the company is on track. If it's no, then it's time to make a change. That's the empowering effect of a well-considered big-idea statement—it makes every employee a stakeholder in the company's mission and gives them the power to monitor and maintain the company's mission. Charles Revson put it beautifully: "At the Revlon factory we make cosmetics; at the drugstore we sell hope."

Here are some other big-idea statements that simply and effectively embody the underlying goals of the company.

Wal-Mart: We give ordinary folks the chance to buy the same things as rich people.

Mary Kay Cosmetics: We give unlimited opportunity to women.

Merck: We preserve and improve human life.

Coca-Cola: We refresh the world.

3M: We solve unsolved problems innovatively.

Walt Disney: We make people happy.

Not one of these big-idea statements refers directly to a product or service. They refer to what the company does. It's not hard to imagine that a sales representative from Merck feels that she can push a little harder on a sales call when she knows that the company's goal is to preserve and improve human life. Any employee of the above companies can ask herself, "Am I doing it now, or not?" and come up with a quick answer. Do you think the asking and the answer affect the bottom line? You bet your boots they do.

Homing In on the Big Idea

I was part of a weekend retreat in Pennsylvania for a national specialty restaurant franchise whose goal was to improve the way they connected with their customers. When we started the process, the company's mission statement said, "We are here to give our customers the best blah, blah, blah, and do it with courtesy and blah, blah, blah, and hold true to blah, blah blah, while always remembering blah, blah blah." No one could remember the whole thing or even tell me what it meant. I had my work cut out for me.

A big idea springs from discovering the true nature of your business. One of the ways I help companies do this is by eliciting criteria from the individuals in charge, one by one and one-on-one. That's really just a fancy way of saying we find out what's important to them—not the obvious stuff, like rewarding the shareholder or offering top-notch customer service or even providing clean toilets. What we have to get at is the company's rock-bottom values and beliefs.

To start this process with the restaurant franchise, I asked each of the company's officers, "What's important to you about a restaurant?" (The starting question always addresses the most basic aspect of the business.) They started listing things, and I scribbled everything down on a chalkboard. Every time it got quiet, I'd just ask, "What else?" until they finally said, "That's it." The only thing I did that was special was use my voice, body language, and word choice to indicate that I was engaged, excited, and curious about where we were going to end up. Here's the abbreviated version:

A company's big idea should pertain to each and every one of its employees.

Me: "What's important to you about a restaurant?"

Him: "Great food, good value, superb service, friendly staff . . ."

Once they finished their lists, I delved deeper into each and every one of these signposts—food, value, service, friendly staff—looking for patterns.

Me: "What's important to you about great food?"

Him: "Makes me feel good when I eat it, gives me time to reflect, then I feel grateful, I enjoy the texture . . ." And so forth.

Me: "What's important to you about good value?"

Him: "I like quality at a good price."

Me: "What else?"

Him: "I like doing business with people I trust . . ."

Then I got them to dig even deeper by discussing each of these new signposts—feeling good, time to reflect, quality, people I trust. Eventually we discovered that just one or two things were at the root of this decision maker's beliefs and values. This process took twenty to thirty minutes and was repeated with all the other decision makers.

In the midafternoon, we brought everybody together and showed them the edited, aggregated list. It included things like: "If I have to wait in line, it has to be worth it." "I like restaurants where you know they actually really care about food." "I like to feel important." "It should smell inviting."

By the end of the day, we had a big idea that excited and inspired everyone, and was so stunningly simple it could trigger the instant mantra "Am I doing it now, or not?" It was, "We make hungry people feel important."

A phrase like this is often trite, obvious, and almost meaningless when viewed from outside the company or corporation that developed it. But when you load up one of these trite big ideas with bricks, mortar, employees, and food, and look at it from the inside, it *is* big. It is something that can change behaviors, attitudes, perceptions, and the bottom line.

A big idea should be short and sweet and trigger the instant mantra "Am I doing it now, or not?"

Is "We make hungry people feel important" memorable? Does it capture the spirit of the organization and point everyone in the same direction? Is it versatile? Does it permit expansion? Yes to all of the above. The company immediately commissioned signs to be designed and stuck on the cash registers at all its outlets. These were a reminder to everyone to stay on track by asking, "Am I doing it now, or not?"

Getting Personal

Just as defining a company's big idea can help keep its staff focused and on track, defining your personal big idea for what you specifically contribute at work can give your professional life more direction and meaning.

Sometimes in the daily grind of things, we undervalue our work. We focus on all that's rote and routine and unglamorous about our work, and lose sight of how we connect to the big picture. But everyone on the planet has an effect on how the world goes around. Ferret out and recognize the value and significance of your contribution and you'll find it increasingly easier to connect with and convince other people. Your work has value, no matter how insignificant it may seem to you.

One of those who homed in on a personal big idea at work is Pat Sullivan, who works for the export division at the Department of Commerce in Ontario. Pat found a phrase that sums up what he does and it makes him proud; it also makes it easier to connect with people. Pat told me, "When I articulated how I made a significant contribution, things seemed to fall in place. Now I know why I get out of bed in the morning." Today, Pat feels like he's part of something bigger than himself. He is motivated—not by a stick or a carrot, but by a sense of belonging. His values are alive.

Before Pat found his big idea, he often found himself almost apologizing for his department. He felt that no one took him or his unit at Commerce seriously. It seemed that few people in the business really understood what his department was doing and how they impacted industry. Pat had a hard time telling anyone how he made a difference in people's lives.

Pat saw himself and the department as a valuable resource to industry, but the work that he and his cohorts did seemed never to be acknowledged, which meant that it never seemed very exciting. It was difficult to crank up his enthusiasm to match that of the entrepreneurs and small-business owners he was there to assist.

EXERCISE

Create Your Own Big-Idea Statement

Find somewhere you won't be disturbed, get a pen and paper out, and warm up by asking yourself a few questions: What is the ultimate result of my work? Why does my organization/job/work/career exist? What difference do I intend to make? What's the *good idea* behind my business? Put down half a dozen words to give a snapshot of you at ten years old, then at twenty. Now you're ready to begin.

You're going to go through the same exercise that the restaurant franchise went through, with the question "What's important to me about . . .?" Start by asking, What's important to *me* about my job? Extract your words,

Recently, though, we got together to talk about his problem. He explained that when his clients were faced with complex jargon—like, "Through our provincial counterparts in embassies and consulates and tourism departments abroad, we are able to identify potential market opportunities and in some cases blah, blah, blah"—the standard response was to glaze over.

After a morning of sharing thoughts and going through the process of refining what I outlined above, he boiled

take note of the signposts, then use them to go to the next level. Keep going until you find out your core values and the things that turn you on.

Next list ten natural gifts and talents—things that have been true about you since you were a child (imagine you're on a game show and you'll receive a thousand dollars for each one you list).

Live with your lists for a few hours or even a few days—however long it takes for a light to go on in your head and for you to say, "Of course! It's so obvious." With guidance, this can be done fairly quickly—on your own it takes a little longer, so take your time. Your brain is busy rearranging the furniture.

down what he does for a living into a simple personal big idea. Pat had a lifelong fascination with solving puzzles, so once he could see his work in this light, his personal big-idea statement became "I solve business puzzles." Now Pat has a sense of direction, he knows how to distinguish and display the department's strength, he knows how to offer the promise of discovering new things, and when he asks himself, "Am I doing it now, or not?" he can always answer with a resounding yes.

Translating Your Big Idea into a Ten-Second Commercial

Your personal big idea is what you tell yourself you do; your ten-second commercial is what you tell others you do. When asked what he does, Pat Sullivan, for example, couldn't go around saying, "I solve business puzzles." People would think he was being silly or coy or worse. But he can say, "I help exporters find new markets, ship their products on time, and get a good night's sleep." The idea behind the ten-second commercial is that once you offer it, the other person is so intrigued that they have to say, "Tell me more." It's an invitation to conversation, to connecting quickly.

Last year I took an assignment in Paris. I thought that I was going to help an automobile rental company work up a big-idea statement. But what I found was a company that needed something for the frontline troops—a ten-second commercial.

I realized this when I spoke to Andrew Harrison, who runs a division of the company that specializes in international rentals. Pick up a car in, say, Lisbon and you can drop it off in Amsterdam—or almost anywhere in western Europe. Two years ago, the company had brought in a consultant to develop a mission statement. After they had analyzed their business, talked with the managers and the employees, and done oodles of research, they turned it in. The mission statement—which management had printed and posted in every agency office around the world—read, "We are dedicated to providing the best value in all of the products and services we provide to our valued customers. Our rates, service, and product quality are—and will remain—second to none."

Andrew summed it up loud and clear. "How does this help me communicate who we are and why we are special? I want to know that if I see the president of Club Med in a bar, I can walk up to him and—*bang*—tell him what I do, who I do it for, and how it makes their life better. Short and sharp and clear. All the things that this isn't."

You've seen a thirty-second commercial on TV. It's so long that you can get up and go to the fridge, let the dog out, put another log on the fire, and check out your hair in

EXERCISE

Your Ten-Second Commercial

Create a brief statement that summarizes what you do, who you do it for, and how it makes their lives easier, better, more fun. Include the benefits you offer clients.

What do you understand? What do you deliver? What do your customers imagine you understand and deliver? If you run a glamorous restaurant, from your point of view you understand food, service, and decor. But your customers might suppose you understand romance. Now you're talking to the imagination and the emotions.

Ask yourself: What difference do I make? List what's important to your customers. What do they want? What do I do for them?

Your ten-second commercial has three parts:

1. What you do.
2. Who you do it for.
3. How it makes their lives better.

It's called a ten-second commercial because you should be able to deliver it in ten seconds. Keep it short and to the point. Keep massaging it until you're sure everyone you offer it to will say, "I'd like to hear more."

the mirror before it's over. Andrew wanted a clear and meaningful explanation of what he really does, how he makes a difference, who it is he helps, and how he makes the world go around—and he needed for it to take up as little of his ninety-second first-impression time as possible.

This is exactly what a ten-second commercial can do. It can be used to make connections at a cocktail party, a trade show, a business lunch, or in an elevator. A ten-second commercial tells the other party what you can offer. It is *not* a sales pitch; it's an engaging, artfully crafted mini-presentation, with a hook and a point, but without any pressure to buy.

Your ten-second commercial should immediately communicate what you do and its value to others.

I asked Andrew and his colleagues, "What does this company understand?" The replies were fast and furious. "How about European roads for starters?" said one. "Hotels and restaurants along the way?" piped the woman on his left. "Flexibility?" offered another. "Freedom," said Andrew, "the freedom of the open road, taking your time." We were on a roll. Reliability, weather, customs, and border crossings came next.

"Wait!" I interrupted, pointing at the words and phrases up on the white board. "Now, there's a thought: flexibility and freedom . . . twenty-four hours a day. How about a ten-second commercial that reads: "We give travelers the freedom to explore Europe twenty-four hours a day"? As with all good ten-second commercials, there was room to adapt it to different circumstances. Suggestions came from around the table: "At a bridal show we could say,

EXERCISE

The "Pub Approach"

What would you say if you saw the client of your dreams sitting in a bar and had only a few seconds while you were ordering a drink to convey your message—to tell her what you do, whom you do it for, and how it makes their lives better?

I spent a lot of time in pubs back in the late 1960s watching Francis Xavier Muldoon deliver his messages quickly, memorably, and succinctly in both formal and informal settings. He called what he did in the latter his "pub approach," adding that he often used it when someone asked him what he did for a living. "The trick," he said, "is to get the other person to say 'yes' before you tell them."

Let's consider Pat's ten-second commercial for his company: "I help exporters find new markets, ship their products on time, and get a good night's sleep."

Here is the "pub approach" to marketing the same company:

"You know how most exporters are always looking to find new markets?"

'We give travelers the freedom to explore Europe to their heart's content.'" "To a traveling delegation, 'We give travelers the freedom to move around Europe twenty-four hours a day.'" There was great enthusiasm in the air—a sure sign that we were onto something.

"Yes."

"Well I help them find those markets and ship their products on time, so they can get a good night's sleep."

Here's the formula and how I apply it to myself and my own business:

You know how . . . companies/people/real estate agents, and so forth . . . "You know how some people have trouble connecting with others?"

Well, we/I . . . "Well, I write books and give speeches to show them how to do it naturally and easily . . ."

So they can . . . "So they can have fun and get more out of life."

Take your ten-second commercial and give it the pub approach. Practice saying it conversationally over and over until you've convinced yourself. Then put it away until you need it.

You can do the same, and make a ten-second commercial for yourself or your company. Start by asking yourself what your company or association understands that others don't. Minolta says it understands offices. Marriott understands friendship, Interflora understands romance. Figure out what you think you or your company understand best, and then ask yourself and your customers what they think you understand and deliver.

A ten-second commercial should make others say, "Tell me more."

The difference between the ten-second commercial and the big idea is that the ten-second commercial doesn't have the "Am I doing it now, or not?" component. What it should have in its place is the irresistible obligation for the other person to ask, "How?" or "Tell me more." This is the test of a great ten-second commercial.

Just as a good idea needs a big-idea statement to give focus, direction, and personality to a company or organization, a ten-second commercial allows you to take the business a stage further—to the people—in a quick, effective, and stimulating way. From a getting-your-idea-to-market point of view, first comes the good idea, then the big idea, and finally the ten-second commercial.

90-Second Summary

The Big Idea

A good idea becomes a big idea with an artfully crafted mission statement—a simple, brief, and memorable explanation of why the organization exists and what difference it makes. The big idea:

- Can give an organization personality. It should be memorable, capture the spirit of the organization, and point everyone in the same direction.
- Does not refer directly to a product or service, but to what the company does. It springs from the true nature of your business.
- Should trigger the instant mantra "Am I doing it now, or not?" The big idea should be the first consideration for any employee making decisions with customers, clients, and colleagues.

The Personal Big Idea

Defining your own personal big idea can give your work life more direction and meaning. This statement conveys the value and essence of what you do. Formulate it in a way that makes sense to you.

The Ten-Second Commercial

A ten-second commercial tells others the value of what you do in a way that invites conversation. Once you offer it, the other person should be so intrigued they say "Tell me more," rather than "Big deal."

- A ten-second commercial has three parts: what you do, who you do it for, and how it makes their lives better.
- Keep your ten-second commercial short and to the point.
- For casual situations, use the pub approach—the "You know how . . . ?/Well, I . . . /So they can . . . " format.

8

Find Your Style

My old mentor F. X. Muldoon put it in the simplest possible terms: "Wear great clothes—more peo-ple will listen to you." Yet despite the fact that we may believe he was right, many of us are so insecure about or indifferent to our appearance or our fashion sense that we don't try any improvements in the wardrobe department until it's too late. We've made our first impression, and it's not that great.

Creating a link between how you look and how you work can give you a competitive edge in business. When people first encounter you, they respond to your attitude—the unspoken message you project as you enter a room. Part of that message is your style or your lack of one. Your present style, or manner, has probably been influenced by those with whom you grew up—your family, your peers, your heroes, even the celebrities you admired. Now is the time to honestly assess what your style says about you and make sure the message is one that benefits you.

Approachable, or Authoritative?

I've shot thousands of fashion ads for major fashion retailers, and we frequently discussed the look we wanted to achieve in terms of whether it was going to be authoritative, approachable, or somewhere in between. These are the North and South Poles of first impressions. Building a professional identity to project a strong first impression must take into account these same boundaries.

Somewhere between the two extremes of approachable and authoritative lies fertile ground where you can nurture an effective professional style. A professional style may or may not conform to current fashion, but it should be an expression of your independence and confidence. Wearing attractive clothes with assurance can positively influence prospective job offers, help secure your long-awaited promotion, or make the difference in landing a multimillion-dollar contract.

Whether you're just walking into a room to shake hands with a new colleague or going up to a podium in front of your entire company, what people see first, as you know, is your attitude. What they see immediately after that is how you put yourself together, your style. (And of course, these two are not separate entities. Your attitude affects your style.)

Taken together, your attitude and personal packaging establish your unspoken credentials. Your authority/approachability quotient determines how other people will initially respond to you when you finally get to open your mouth. Think of a sliding scale of work attire with blue jeans (the pants of the people) at one end and very expensive, custom-made suits (the togs of the toffs) at the other. Of course, you don't have to get stuck at one end or the other. Most people find a comfortable spot that borrows and combines elements from both ends. (Remember the way I combined an authoritative top with an approachable bottom when I approached strangers on the street for *The New York Times* article?)

Make sure what you wear is projecting the message you want to send.

For example, a man with a *serious* attitude and a set of bankers' pinstripes to match presents a facade of total authority. But if you add a pair of bright red suspenders to that pinstriped suit, the businessman immediately becomes more approachable. How sure am I about this? Well, who's going to feel threatened by Larry King while he's keeping his pants up with his trademark suspenders? They make him look like the intelligent good sport that he is.

A woman can present the same *serious* facade of authority by showing up in the modern business uniform of dark suit and sensible heels. But like the suspender-wearing banker, she can show her approachability by

Dress for Success

Do looks really matter? The answer is yes. Image has a very real impact on your ability to convince people, and like it or not, wardrobe plays a big part in those crucial first ninety seconds when you're scrambling to make a connection.

Creating the first impression that you desire is all about imagination. Muldoon told me, "Dress for the job you want—not the job you have. Let your boss picture you giving important presentations, not flogging classifieds over the phone. Use your wardrobe as a way to present your personality with style."

Your personal style will continue to exert a strong influence over career advancement because, yes, if we don't actually know the author, we do judge a book by its cover. Putting it another way, the great doyenne of fashion Coco Chanel said, "If a person is poorly dressed, you notice their clothing; but if they are impeccably dressed, you notice the person."

adding a flash of color with a bright scarf or a piece of whimsical jewelry.

These imaginative touches have a persuasive impact on the first impression you choose to create because they offer a *controlled glimpse* of your personality—they suggest what you'll be like when people get to know you.

The *KFC* of Fashion

Say you want to spiff up your look. How do you figure out what clothes or accessories to buy? Do you look at your peers? Do you look at the boss? Do you look to the fashion pages? What's a good basic way to figure out what works?

You can begin by asking some *KFC* questions: Where do I want to fit on the approachability/authority scale? (The middle is not a good place to be—err on the side of authority.) What do I want my clothing to communicate to others? How much of a chameleon do I want to be? Is there an aspect of my personality that I want my personal packaging to emphasize? Does my current wardrobe do this? Take into account your physical characteristics and make sure the look you're creating works with them.

Next, get savvy. Read the top fashion magazines in your country. Study international publications, especially the French, English, and Italian men's and women's

(continued on page 156)

EXERCISE

Find Your Style

What is your current look saying about you? Is your image at work what you want it to be? Here are seven questions you should ask yourself about the way you dress for work.

1. **Do I look like a professional in the eye of the beholder?**
   Attention to detail makes you look like a professional. If you look professional, you often feel professional. There are many business cultures where being immaculate is considered the hallmark of the warrior. *Tip:* A monochromatic color scheme is the most sophisticated way of dressing. Proof positive—Giorgio Armani has made a fortune dressing people this way. Wearing different shades of the same palette is soothing.
2. **Does my grooming match my wardrobe?**
   Is your hair clean and well-cut? Are your nails neat and tidy? Do you smell too much of perfume or cologne—or, worse, not enough deodorant? And remember, even the smell of secondhand smoke can torpedo you.
3. **Is my clothing well-maintained?**
   Attention to detail is key. Are your clothes properly pressed? No spots, no loose threads, no loose buttons? Are your shoes polished? Would you wear it on TV—close-up?
4. **Are my clothes out-of-date?**
   Some clothes go out of style faster than others. You can

play it safe with a wardrobe that's more perpetual—a cashmere sweater or a navy suit—or you can be trendy. Just remember, if you go for an up-to-the-minute look, be prepared to replace your clothes frequently. In business, when your clothes are out-of-date, *you* are out-of-date.

5. **Does my footwear send the right message?**
   One of the first things men look at in women, and women in men, is their footwear. Are the shoes worn, cracked, dirty, or out-of-date? Do they match the outfit? Make a statement? My red shoes add a playful note to an otherwise straightforward style.
6. **Are my clothes too busy or distracting?**
   Can people concentrate on your ideas without being distracted or overwhelmed by your sartorial splendor? What overall message is your wardrobe signaling to others?
7. **Does my clothing give other people ammunition to criticize me?**
   Do your clothes fit properly? Are they too big or too small? Size doesn't matter—fit matters. Do you look clean? Have you paid attention to detail? Are you tastefully dressed and is your overall image congruent with your personality and your ideas?

Remember, your clothes convey a lot about you. Invest in a wardrobe with the same care as you invest your savings. There will be a payoff.

fashion monthlies. These often show higher fashion than most of us wear on a regular basis, but they can give you a sense of style. Keep an eye out for items that match the image you've created for yourself.

Third, connect with people—talk to fashion-conscious friends and family members. Ask advice from those whose sense of style you admire. (One caveat about advice from friends and family: Be sure to talk to those who are willing to see you change. Some of your loved ones might want you to succeed but might have a hard time parting with the image of you that they know and love.) If those in your circle aren't going to do the trick, hire a consultant—or go to a good store (you don't have to buy anything), try stuff on, and get opinions, lots of them. Many high-end department stores provide in-house personal shoppers gratis. These people are a bit like fashion stylists—they help you find the right look for the right occasion. Once they get to know you, personal shoppers save you time. They will get together three to five ensembles in advance and have them waiting for you. It's their job to present you at your best and steer you clear of any inappropriate look. Besides giving you

Consider buying a high-quality briefcase or handbag. The right accessory can make you look better-dressed than you are.

a clean, fresh appearance, they can also help you pull together and update your existing wardrobe. In addition, locate and develop a relationship with the best hairdresser and shoe store you can afford.

Be prepared to spend on quality. You are making an investment that can boost your personal share value. Invest in clothes that are an excellent fit and favor your proportions. Find colors that make you look healthy, fresh, and vibrant, and develop a style to accentuate your personality and your potential. If you can't afford the most expensive tailored suits, splurge on accessories. Buy the very best purse, scarf, briefcase, or shoes you can afford. When we shot low-end merchandise, we frequently used props that cost much more than the outfits, and it made a tremendous difference. The right accessory can make you look better dressed than you are.

Acting the Part

Two years after my adventures in London with Francis Xavier Muldoon, I found myself in Cape Town, South Africa, reporting for work on my first day with the *Cape Times,* the city's morning newspaper. I had been hired to sell advertising space on "special projects"—a euphemism for problem areas. Rich in the lessons learned and digested from the maestro back in England, I was optimistic about my prospects. Following F. X.'s advice, I had invested in a professional wardrobe. I looked more like my boss than like my office mate.

What an unforgettable first day it turned out to be. My boss, Mr. Eckerman, called me into his office to brief me for my first assignment. He took a features section out of his filing cabinet, laid it down on his desk, and spun it around so I could take it in. "Twice a year we bring out this fashion supplement, but the advertisers don't seem to like it. I want you to go out there and find out why."

My reply was brash, heartfelt, and enthusiastic. "I can tell you why right now. It's because the pictures are dreadful. I could take better pictures than that."

"You think so." He looked me right in the eye.

I didn't flinch. "Yes."

He pursed his lips, nodded his head, twitched his mustache; and a twenty-five-year career in fashion and advertising photography was launched. "Okay," he said, "you're on." Just like that!

Mamma mia! What had I gotten myself into? I didn't know the first thing about photography. I didn't even own a camera! Fortunately, before I became too overwhelmed, Francis Xavier piped up on my shoulder, "Find the best people you can."

With the help of the paper's fashion editor, I found the best models in town, the best hair stylist, the best makeup artist, the best stylist (the person who dresses and accessorizes the talent), and a seasoned photographer with his own studio. Until I met him I'd never even been inside a commercial photo studio before.

I confided my innocence to the stylist and she discreetly told me every good move she'd ever seen a photographer make. And she'd seen plenty. Most of what I knew about fashion photography I'd gotten from seeing the classic 1966 movie *Blow-Up,* about a scruffy young fashion photographer who rode around London in a Rolls-Royce and shot wild fashion spreads in his studio. Once again I was a chameleon. I dressed like the guy in *Blow-Up,* and did what the stylist had told me, and everyone assumed I knew much more than I did. I got in the mood (adjusted my attitude to *mischievous*) and quickly figured out what I wanted. I told the models where to stand and got them in the mood—attitude is infectious. I even took some of the pictures with the photographer's guidance.

We did twenty-four setups that day, including five exteriors. In some shots the models looked more formal and authoritative; in others they were more casual and approachable. I learned how tailored clothing, for both men and women, could make the models look important, credible, and persuasive, while the more casual clothing made the same models appear more accessible, cooperative, and relaxed. Of course, they adjusted their attitudes to reflect the desired mood.

All the professionals did what they were hired to do. I learned by doing, directing the models where to stand and how to feel. When you take pictures, you can't tell people to "look happy" or "look important"—you have to make them feel it. And I discovered that that was something I could do, and do well: I'd get into their skin and set up synchronizing patterns with body language. "Mm, like this. Ah. Shoulder here, like this." Then I'd use my voice. I'd adopt a party voice and say, "Great!" Then a sizzling voice: "Great." Then an outrageous voice: "Great."

When the sixteen-page supplement was published the following Saturday, it included a small text box in the center of the opening spread that said "Photos by Nick Boothman." What a buzz! I may not have taken every photo, but I brought it all together and made it happen.

Why am I telling you this story? To show there is a connection between attitude, personality, and packaging. When they are in synch, together they send a strong message of confidence, and confidence begets good things. When I walked into my boss's office that first day, I felt that I looked like a million bucks and exuded the self-assurance to match. During the shoot, dressing the part gave me a boost of confidence that I sorely needed, considering my inexperience. Plus, I learned firsthand that day the degree to which clothes and attitude affect the way you're perceived. The very same models looked dramatically different in their various outfits and moves. To me, what it boiled down to was this: Dress so you feel at the top of your game, in a way that makes you feel you can conquer the world.

Should You Change Your Existing Image?

Scott, a friend of mine, changed careers to become a Realtor. He confided, "I had no problem getting my license, but I'm having no luck at all getting people to list their properties with me. How do I get people to trust me?" Scott had invested almost a year of his life and a considerable amount of money in achieving his paper credentials. I suggested he invest two weeks and a little more money to buff up his image.

First, we talked about approachability and authority. If you are considering trusting a stranger to sell your house, that stranger had better look, sound, feel, smell, and taste like they know what they're doing. You want him to have lots of authority, but you also want him to be approachable. You need to be able to talk to him easily. We went through the questions I asked on pages 154–155 to determine what he wanted his personal style to communicate to others.

Scott knew he wanted to make people trust and respect him, but he still didn't know exactly what look to adopt. We talked about the different kinds of looks that might work for him, and came up with a number of ideas. Then, in a high-flying mood, Scott came up with the idea of trying a different style of dressing each day for a week, with the proviso that each style was reasonable for him. He decided on Monday he'd look "sporty," Tuesday he'd try "Wall Street," Wednesday he'd be "preppy," Thursday he'd go for a "country" look, and Friday he'd cast himself as "the poet." Where he found the clothes was up to him, but they had to be quality.

Scott bought magazines, spoke to sales associates in clothing stores, and paid new attention to his hair, his shoes, and his accessories. On top of this, he agreed to spend some time alone, imagining how he would look, sound, feel, and smell in each of these styles. (Capturing your own imagination is an important part of the process of connecting with who you are.) I provided Scott with a list of really useful *(warm, enthusiastic, confident)* and really useless *(rude, conceited, impatient)* attitudes and asked him to link one or two useful ones to each style. These would help him define and characterize each style. Besides doing all this research, imagining, and shopping, Scott agreed to maximize his "style week" by working harder and smarter than he ever had before. Scott was already a hardworking and determined guy by anyone's standards, but he had decided to make this his go-for-it week.

I asked Scott to be aware of how he felt and the kind of response he was getting from others as he went through each and every day of this week. I wanted him to take special notice of those moments when he felt people were taking him seriously and trusting him. The proof of his success would be whether or not he improved his record in landing new listings. We agreed not to speak again until he had some concrete feedback.

A few weeks went by, and one day, out of the blue, he phoned me. The first thing I noticed was the enthusiasm in his voice. I scribbled down notes as he told me the country look—corduroy pants, sweaters, and tweeds—suited him to a T. (This was no big surprise to me, since Scott was as kinesthetic as you can get.) He said he'd always felt uncomfortable and cramped in business suits, and he didn't feel like he was working when he was in casuals. "Right away on the country day, I hit my style" (kinesthetic language).

He discovered that his new style of dressing changed his style of thinking and operating—not just when it came to landing new listings, but also when dealing with colleagues in the office and (much more to his delight) when negotiating with other agents. He had previously admitted

EXERCISE

Seeing Your Image

Come up with two or three words that effectively capture the image you'd like to project—innovative, modern, reliable, conservative, adventurous, bold, progressive, traditional, professional, friendly, and so forth. Invest some time in a library or bookstore that carries American, English, French, and Italian fashion periodicals. Think about shape, color, and textures.

Now imagine yourself five years down the road toward success. You are going to create a future memory, a specific moment in time when you are successful. Maybe you are in your private jet on the way to open yet another restaurant in Paris. Perhaps you're sitting around the breakfast table laughing with your kids and deciding to take Monday off. Make your image reasonable: Chances are you won't be in a private jet if you see yourself as a kindergarten teacher. And it's unlikely you'll be a croupier in Sin City if you've got three small kids at home.

to occasionally being a confused and uneasy victim of certain mind games perpetrated by a few of the more seasoned agents when getting down to the short strokes. Now his newfound style gave him an air of affable authority that he hadn't had before. It disguised his inexperience and lack of confidence. "I'm not as obvious as I used to be. People take me more seriously."

Next, imagine yourself in the bedroom or dressing room of your future home. Open your wardrobe of the future. It's empty. Your clothes haven't been delivered yet. Now, close your eyes and see this successful you five years from now. Ask yourself, How will I know when I'm successful? What will it look like, feel like, sound like, smell like, and taste like, specifically? Who will be there with me? How will my life change to accommodate this success? How will I look? How do I want to look? Start mentally filling the wardrobe. Now, open your eyes. It's time to take the first step toward creating a look for yourself.

You can start the process right now. Begin by determining where you want to fit on the approachability/authority scale. Then establish whether you are more comfortable as a casual or formal type of person. Bear in mind the conventional confines and requirements of your occupation or profession. When you're ready to take the next step, call in the professionals.

Since the transformation, he'd done six deals and changed offices. "I feel like I'm working at a cut above where I was before, and people take notice of me," Scott said.

You don't have to go as far as Scott did to find the image that works for you. If you feel you could do with a little sprucing up, try the exercise described above.

Birds of a Feather Flock Together

Have you ever noticed that some of the people you come across in business prefer to make themselves *look like a million bucks,* while others just seem to enjoy *making a statement* with their choice of clothing, and yet others would rather dress to *feel comfortable?* That's right—we're talking visual, auditory, and kinesthetic.

What's more, you'll probably find that if you're the sort of person for whom being visually immaculate is important, you'll be comfortable socializing and working with people who dress like you. By the same token, those folks whose personal dressing style favors loose, textured, or just plain old comfortable clothing will be attracted to others who dress similarly, *and* they'll probably discover they have more than just a dress code in common. And those with a flair for making a personal statement with their wardrobe will easily find inspiration in one another's company.

Your plumage is like a sensory-biased uniform, attracting others who share the same sensory preferences. But a word of caution here. Make sure you're not fooling yourself into believing you have good people skills just because you can get on with people who are like you: Eagle with eagles, penguin with penguins, turkey with turkeys is the easy, unconscious way to semisuccess.

To truly succeed, you must learn how to connect with the people who are not really that much like you and don't favor the same sensory preferences as you. Socially, the friends we choose probably do share those same preferences. We tend to choose friends who are like us and share much in common, but that's the point—we choose our friends. In business that's not the case. We can't always choose who we do business with, so we have to make adaptations to accommodate those who are unlike us. Yes, birds of a feather do flock together, and it's good for friendships—but bad for business.

You can learn a lot about other people's connecting styles by reading the sensory bias of their personal packaging. Pay attention to what their clothes tell you about their sensory preferences, and use it to your advantage. Speak in a language that will resonate with them; address their priorities.

The way people package themselves can tell you a lot about them. Read the signals and use them to connect.

Packaging yourself in a way that reflects potential and confers authority can put you on the fast track to making new and unexpected business connections. Style begins with a useful attitude and ends with a useful appearance. Just as you must be congruent in your body language and your words to be perceived as sincere and trustworthy, so you need to also pay attention to the congruence, or harmony, between the characteristics of your body, your personality, and your clothing. You'll feel and act your best when your style reflects your best—the you when you're at the top of your game. Remember, you are always communicating, and the validation of communication is the response it gets. This communication template also applies to your business style. Be aware of how others respond to you. If they aren't responding the way you want, then change what you do (or how you look) until you get what you want.

Ultimately, style comes from within. It comes from the person inside you that others may not see. Your style is that person, refined by how you think, how you act and react, how you dress, and what you do. Package your personality to showcase your potential. Create a link between the internal you, with your skills and capabilities, and the external world, where you contribute and make a living. And do it in a way that establishes your approachability, your authority, and your credibility. You will give yourself a strong competitive edge in business.

90-Second Summary

Find Your Style

When people first respond to you, they respond to your attitude—the unspoken message you project. Part of that message is your style. To make a great first impression, develop an individual style that is an expression of independence and confidence.

- An effective professional style balances approachability with authority.
- Decide on an image you want to project. Ask yourself: What personality style do I have? What do I want my clothing to communicate to others about my strengths and my personality? Does my current wardrobe do this?
- Dress for the job you want—not the job you have.
- Remember, when you are poorly dressed, people notice your clothing; when you are perfectly dressed, they notice *you.*
- If you decide you want to project a different image, keep experimenting and changing until you find a look that works for you.

- If you need help, consider calling in a professional, such as a consultant or a personal shopper.
- Notice how you feel and be aware of how others respond to you.

Part Four

Building Relationships

Other people are your greatest resource. Build relationships with them and they can offer you business, inspiration, promotion, and any form of cooperation you can name. Fail to build relationships and these same people can easily hold you back from the success you hope for.

Learning to successfully socialize and network, and even schmooze, is in part like learning your lines in a play. First you get a feel for the script. Then you divide it into small chunks, which you learn and absorb one at a time, with the director's guidance. Once your lines are memorized and you have a good feel for the material, then you forget what the director told you, put your own spin on it, and let your personality shine through.

9
Open the Lines of Communication

Have you ever noticed that some people can arrive at a meeting, a conference, or a party and, within a few seconds of arriving, seem to be everywhere and with everyone at the same time? And they make this miracle look natural and easy. For these people, every business and social event represents an opportunity to meet people, network, and expand their business reach. But take heart. These opportunities exist for everybody.

Sure, there are people for whom socializing appears to come naturally, but in reality it's a skill that you can learn. The talents of these socially gifted individuals can become your own. I have broken down their seemingly effortless socializing skills into a series of steps that anyone can adopt.

These steps can be applied in all situations and will facilitate your connecting, whether it's during a coffee break or at a meeting with new clients, an industry social function, or a sales conference where you're seeing people you see only once or twice a year.

Whether you're meeting someone for the first time or the fifth, what follows is a tried and tested procedure for greeting people in the vast majority of situations. I have divided this procedure into five parts:

1. **Open**
2. **Eye**
3. **Smile**
4. **Speak**
5. **Synch**

Whenever it's possible, stand up to greet someone. If you're at work, stand up and come around your desk to greet all your visitors, whether they're clients, new colleagues, or associates. Like turning your heart toward the person you're meeting, this is a way of removing barriers and opening yourself up to the person and the conversation. It's awkward if you leave the desk between you from the moment they enter until the time they're ready to leave. Obviously, if it's not appropriate to stand, don't, but as a general rule you should rise to the occasion.

Open: The first part of the greeting is to open your attitude and your body. For this to work properly, you must have already adopted a really useful attitude. This is the time to be mindful of it, to feel it, and be aware of it. Point your heart at the person you are meeting and check to be sure you have nothing covering your chest—no hands, arms, clipboards, or other work paraphernalia. I always make a point of making sure my hands are visible. It disarms the other person's subconscious fight-or-flight response by showing them that I have nothing to hide.

Eye: Be the first to make eye contact. Immediately make a mental note of the color of the person's eyes.

Smile: Be first to smile. Let your smile reflect your attitude. A great smile shows that you are confident, honest, and enthusiastic. (If you smile before you meet their eyes, that's fine. The effect's the same. This all happens in a matter of a few seconds, so just be comfortable and let your attitude show through.)

Speak: Whether it's "Hey!" or "Hi!" or "Ho!" or "Hello!" greet the person with pleasing tonality. If you're meeting someone for the first time, get your name in first—"Hello, I'm Joanna"—take the lead. If a handshake is appropriate, it usually happens during the exchange of names. Unfortunately, far too often, as we try to get our hands together and try to remember to squeeze hard enough but not too hard, sensory overload results and what our ears hear, our brain can't retain. This is the moment that makes you forget the names of so many of the people you meet. Stop. Slow down just a little. Listen carefully to the other person's name.

Synch: By "synch" I mean: Begin immediately synchronizing the person's body language and overall voice characteristics. If you are talking to more than one person, turn toward each person you're addressing in turn. When I synchronized the five bicycle couriers, I turned to each one as I engaged them and synched with them. So synch up with each person you're meeting, even if it's just for a few seconds.

The greeting rules apply even when someone else has taken the lead. You still need to adjust your attitude, make eye contact, smile, open your body language, respond, and synchronize.

The Handshake

I know it's a cliché, but it's true. When you shake hands, people make an immediate judgment about your character and level of confidence. A handshake should be firm, quick, and respectful, not too hard, and definitely not too soft. If you're not sure: err on the hard side. (But if the recipient's eyes start to bulge, it's probably an indication that your handshake is a bit too firm. Alternatively, if she looks like she wants to wipe her hand on a towel after you've shaken it, then you were probably giving the wet noodle special—yuk!) The bottom line is that a handshake should not distract from the introduction.

Small Talk: The WD-40 of Interpersonal Communication

Magda spent two months working to gather the human resources department heads of twenty-eight specialty care clinics at one meeting so they could review a new set of protocols. After several face-to-face meetings with some of them, Magda's boss called her into his office and said, "I have some good news and some bad news. They've agreed to get together. But they don't want to work with you."

Magda was shattered and confused. She came to me for help. I soon learned this wasn't the first time something like this had happened to her. Magda was a bright, presentable, no-nonsense woman. At first her tales made no sense. Then something struck me.

"How do you feel about small talk?" I asked her.

"Don't do it. Can't stand it," she replied.

I suggested that her attitude made her appear rather like a brand-new Jaguar car that had come straight off the production line but was missing its paint. Perfect in every way—but uncomfortable to be around.

"Small talk," I told her, "is like the WD-40 of interpersonal communication. It just makes things go more smoothly."

Small talk is casual chitchat about nothing in particular, but it greases the social wheels and enables people who don't know each other well (or at all) to learn about one another in a safe, nonconfrontational way. It's also easy to do. You can start with softball comments about the weather. Or you can ask about the person's commute to wherever you are. You can comment on sports or something that's taken place in the neighborhood, or offer a genuine compliment on an unusual piece of clothing or accessory.

As you continue to interact, you might ask questions about what the person likes to do in his spare time. Or where she is from. You can chat about pop culture: the latest celebrity scandal, a best-selling book, a hot new movie, who's going to win *American Idol.* An easy and natural comment about the occasion or location followed by an open question works wonders. You don't need to agonize over sparkling opening lines—just say something and then add a tag question ("Isn't it?" or "Don't they?" or "Doesn't it?").

Keep the conversation light, and stay way from anything political or sexual. Pick up on pointers and free information (see page 185). Expand on what you already know about each other. Talk about who you know and look for common ground. Show you are genuinely interested.

Make sure the other person does at least half of the talking. Remember to shut up and listen. Listen with your eyes and your ears.

Facilitating—Introducing Others

If you introduce your boss to a friendly media contact, or a client to someone who can help improve his manufacturing process, or a colleague to someone who can advise her on a better way to get her kids through college, you build more personal capital for yourself. The more accomplished you become at facilitating valid introductions, the more you'll be noticed as someone with strong and fluid people skills. Get good at introducing people. It'll make you stand out from the crowd, and people will think you have loads of confidence.

As F. X. Muldoon put it, "Introductions are an important part of business. Learn to handle them graciously, and you display the hallmark of a polished business professional."

When you have to introduce other people, don't keep them waiting. Step up and get on with it. Not only will you need to know their names, but good business etiquette demands that you sort out the pecking order. The smaller cheese gets introduced to the bigger cheese. It's always, "Mr. President, I'd like to introduce Bruce Harris." Never, "Bruce Harris, I'd like to introduce the president."

If there are no hierarchical considerations, introduce

by age. If you're making introductions in a group and you encounter someone you don't know, take the initiative—introduce yourself and say, "My name is So-and-so. I don't believe we've met," and then include this new acquaintance of yours in the stream of introductions.

Engineering Introductions

If you see someone you'd like to meet at a gathering, ask your host or a mutual friend to introduce you. But don't leave things to chance. Instead, prepare your own ten-second commercial ahead of time by telling your introducer what to say—your name, perhaps where you're from, and what you do for a living—whatever you think would most interest the person you're being introduced to. An informed introduction will come off a lot better than "Margot, this is Jamie. Jamie, Margot."

If you really want to impress, ask your host to tell you one or two interesting (but not too personal) things about the person you want to meet before he or she introduces you. Then, when you do connect, you can say, "Peter tells me you spent last month cycling through Guatemala. What was your biggest challenge? What inspired you to go?" Knowing something specific and recent about the person you're meeting allows you to bypass small talk and get to a more personal footing faster.

The Three-Second Rule

In a perfect world there would always be someone available to make the introduction and a familiar, emotionally comfortable space within which to interact—a meeting, a lunch, a networking group, a fund-raiser, or a class. Researchers call these settings "closed fields." They are a place where everyone has the opportunity to meet others and the expectation that they'll do so. Meeting people in a comfortable closed field, with an introduction from a mutual acquaintance, gives you an automatic conversational opening, even if it's as simple as "How do you know Bob?" or "How did you get involved with this project?" It also makes it more likely that you will share interests, values, and tastes, enabling you to establish rapport quickly and effectively.

Don't let your inhibitions prevent you from meeting people. Count to three then introduce yourself.

There are bound to be times, though, when you see someone you'd like to meet in an open field, like a convention, a product knowledge session, an executive lounge, or aboard a commuter train. For most of us, this can be a daunting situation. After all, from the earliest age our parents told us never to talk to strangers, and the mere thought of doing so immobilizes many of us. Let's make a new rule, though. While "Don't talk to strangers" is a great watchword for kids, it's nonsensical for adults, and is actually counterproductive.

It takes a lot of guts to approach a stranger and start talking. But there are times when you must act now or never see the person again. Here's a natural and easy guideline to connecting on a personal level at, say, a dental convention. With a little modification, these steps apply equally at work, at a trade show, or wherever opportunity presents itself.

1. Harness the Three-Second Rule. Don't overthink it! Take a deep breath, count to three, and adopt a great attitude—curious, enthusiastic, calm are all good. It's simple: When you see someone you want to talk to, say to yourself, "One, two, three," and walk over, without hesitating. The key is to make your move within three seconds. Don't let your brain take over and start coming up with excuses. Make sure your body language is open (no crossed arms or hands in pockets). Then seize the moment, count to three, and approach calmly.

2. Say something. You could begin with a casual statement tailored to the situation (perhaps something about the city or the weather) followed by an open question (one that begins with who, what, where, why, when, or how). The goal is to select a topic that directs attention away from the two of you. If it's appropriate, use a prop, like a catalog, to deflect attention. Pick up the catalog and wait a few seconds. Then casually ask a question, like "Do you know anything about this company?"

3. Build trust. Once you've opened a line of communication, you need to demonstrate integrity and gain credibility quickly. The best way to build trust is by linking yourself to the event by talking about your work, school, or community involvement—something local and reliable. You might say "My office is Montreal, and I come here almost every year."

4. Hunt for common ground. Be on the lookout for opportunities to say "Me, too" (or "What a coincidence," or "Funny you should say that"). Be honest and sincere.

5. Evaluate. Chatting for twenty seconds is long enough to tell if a person is interested in talking. If it's not going well, politely exit the conversation and don't be discouraged. Be fearless and calm, and detach yourself from the outcome.

6. Synchronize. If you feel a connection, escalate the intensity by subtly mirroring the person's overall body

EXERCISE

The Three-Second Rule in Action

In the following scenarios, use the details of the situation, assume you have rapport, and decide what you would say. Come up with a conversational statement, and follow it with an open question.

1. It's raining as you leave the store. Several people are waiting under the awning for the rain to let up a bit because they, like you, have no umbrella. You are standing near someone and, "One, two, three," you say . . .

2. You're at work, and you decide to walk outside for your break because it's a beautiful afternoon. You notice a new hire whom you haven't met. "One, two, three," you approach and say . . .

3. On your way to work you stop to pick up a cup of coffee and notice someone you've seen in another department. He/she is also getting ready to pour a cup. "One, two, three," you say . . .

position and voice (tone, speed, and volume). If the person speaks slowly and quietly, do the same.

7. Engage. If you are still chatting after two minutes, you can take the encounter wherever you want, or ask for a phone number or e-mail address. This can be a difficult thing to do, so if you don't feel like coming right out and asking, then pick up on something you've been talking about and offer to send a link or some information if the person will share an e-mail address. When you ask for contact information, remain calm and look the person in the eye. If the person agrees to your request, take down the information or exchange business cards. If your request is rejected, then say politely, "It was nice chatting with you," and go about your business with your confidence intact.

Free Information

The first few seconds of any meeting is rich in opportunity. We can use the natural human tendency to synchronize and reciprocate behavior in many ways, including obtaining free information.

In a controlled business situation—as opposed to, say, bumping into strangers on the street—if I say "Good morning," you'll probably say "Good morning," or something similar, right? What if I shake your hand and say "Good morning, I'm Jeff"? The expectation is now in place for you to respond with comparable information: "Hello, I'm Janet." If you just say "Hello" without proffering your name, I can reasonably suggest you give it to me, either with something as simple as an inquiring look or as devastating as "And you are?"

The Name Game

As companies grow and become national or even international, many people face the chilling experience of frantically trying to remember who's who on those few occasions when large groups get together. If you see someone you've met before but don't remember their name, make the first move and reintroduce yourself. Jog their memory with a line like, "Good morning, I'm Elizabeth Davis. We met recently at the Cougar Global launch. It's good to see you again."

If this were a game of tennis, it would be like putting the ball in the other person's court. The person either knows she is supposed to reciprocate and send it back and will do so naturally, or you can encourage her to do so. The point is that you have to set the person up to reciprocate. Within reason, you can include multiple tags in your own introduction. "Hello, I'm Jeff. I live in Beaverton and I read about this meeting in the local paper." The circuits are laid. Either the other person will respond in kind with her own information or you can nudge her along with a few nods and encouraging words. What you end up with is information about the other person that can be used to rev up a conversation and really connect.

The Hunt for Common Ground

At the heart of the process of establishing instant rapport is a hunt for common ground. We like people who are like us. To discover we share the same interest in movies, clothes, vacations, restaurants, TV shows, football, or skydiving is to find a mutual bond that allows us to share the familiarity of language and experience and accelerate the feeling that we already know, understand, and trust the other person.

The quicker you can find things in common with the person or people you are connecting with, the faster rapport can be established. Venture beyond "Looks like rain" and "How about them Red Sox, eh?" by using a snippet of personal or business small talk to set the agenda. "They're retooling the engine plant, so we're up to our eyeballs in scheduling. How has it affected you?"

To find common ground, ask questions that spark the imagination.

Even if you don't have a shared engine plant or the like in common, the easiest way to get someone talking is to ask them what they think about something. If you're at a convention, ask them what they think about the transportation, the hotel, the hours, their first impressions of the place. "Is this your first trip? What's your initial impression?" "What do you think of the view from the observation deck?"—anything to get them going. Another rapport-creating question is "How did you get started?" As in "How did you get started in sales?" or "What led you to finance?" This is a story that everybody has to tell, and it's almost guaranteed to get a conversation started.

As soon as you find common ground, you find direction and momentum, the comfort level expands, and you can start to relax a little.

However, skip the step of finding common ground and you're playing with fire. At a recent executive seminar, I was told the following horror story that shows many of the ways you can miss one opportunity after another to connect. The players here are Lucinda, an ambitious young analyst at a brokerage company, and Dianne, a more senior analyst and her company's best presenter. Lucinda has invited Dianne to lunch in the hopes she will help her prepare for a crucial presentation.

"Do you know anything about Mongolian food?" Lucinda asked Dianne as she ushered her from their table to the buffet at the center of the restaurant she'd chosen for their lunch. Without giving Dianne the chance to answer, she continued on, "It's really great. Here, take more. Let me put it on the plate for you." Lucinda tweezered heaps of raw pork and chicken onto Dianne's plate. "I know you think it looks greedy, but the food shrinks so much when they cook it."

"I have been to a Mongolian restaurant before," Dianne declared.

"Have you been here?" Lucinda asked, then continued. "The big stars eat here. Do you know who came in the other day?"

As they got back to their table, Lucinda was still talking. And while they ate, she kept talking nervously about other restaurants, celebrities she'd seen, the gym she went to.

"So what's all this about a presentation?" Dianne interrupted her.

"I have to make this presentation in two weeks. It's the biggest assignment my boss has given me so far, and I can't afford to mess it up. I'm hoping you can give me some pointers."

"Who's it for?"

"I can't tell you that, it's confidential," Lucinda said, looking around the restaurant as if she was afraid someone might hear.

"You can't tell me?" Dianne asks incredulously.

Lucinda nods, saying, "My boss doesn't want me to talk about it."

"A good presentation starts with knowing your audience, and *you can't tell me?* How do you expect me to help you?" Dianne looked like she was ready for this lunch to be over.

"Look, everybody tells me you're the best there is at making this sort of presentation. I just thought that I could get some of your secrets . . ." Lucinda's voice trailed off as she saw the look on Dianne's face.

"Oh, really?" Dianne looked at her watch. "You want me to tell you how I do things and what I've learned so maybe you can take over my job one day?"

Lucinda thought that one over for a moment. When she saw Dianne glance at her watch a second time, she

EXERCISE

The Hunt for Common Ground

For one morning, practice finding common ground with strangers or people you hardly know. Try to find it in less than sixty seconds. Throughout the afternoon, do it in less than thirty seconds.

Ask questions that send a person straight into his or her imagination. These don't have to be odd or unusual. They simply can't be closed-ended, like "Have you been here before?" Rather, ask "What do you think about this convention space?" We call them *trance questions* because for a split second people glaze over as they go looking for the answer. A funny thing happens to many said in a very small voice, "If you don't have time now, maybe you could send me an e-mail?"

Signaling for the bill, Dianne said calmly, "I don't think so."

Me, me, me. Lucinda was entirely wrapped up in herself. She was nervous about asking for help and overcompensated by babbling away until she had completely infuriated the woman who could help her. She was so busy babbling that she didn't offer Dianne a single chance to connect. When Dianne mentioned she'd been to a Mongolian restaurant before, that could have been a

folks when they go into their imagination at your request: There's a kind of intimacy that happens. It's as though they think you can see, hear, feel, taste, and smell the same things they can inside their mind. Ask someone about the last really funny movie they saw and watch their expression and demeanor change.

Actively listen and observe how others find common ground. Collect your own supply of questions. You can't use the same questions for everyone, because we all have differing sensibilities, but you'd be surprised at how many people you can reach with no more than three or four good questions.

bridge to common ground. "I'm so pleased. What do you like? How long ago?"—but Lucinda missed it. Or Lucinda could have acknowledged her problems and shown her vulnerability by saying something like "I want something from you because I admire you" or "Can I let you in on a secret? I'm involved in this wonderful project and I'm quite nervous. You know what they're thinking, 'Can a woman get it right?'" or "I know this stuff, but somehow I freeze when I present. Dianne, you're a legend here. Your presentations score a 10 plus. Could you help me?"

These women could have ended up as allies but Lucinda made a poor first impression, made no use of feedback, showed no flexibility, and used no imagination. Lucinda failed to find common ground and failed to connect.

90-Second Summary

The Greeting

Socializing is a skill that comes more naturally to some, but everyone can learn the skills necessary to make connections with new people. The tried-and-true procedure for greeting people can be divided into five parts:

- **Open.** Open your attitude and your body. Point your heart at the person you are meeting.
- **Eye.** Be first to make eye contact. Make a mental note of the color of the person's eyes.
- **Smile.** Be the first person to smile. Let your smile reflect your attitude and show you are confident, honest, and enthusiastic.
- **Speak.** In a warm, friendly voice, greet the person. Give your name first. "Hey, I'm Joanna." Take the lead. Make it a practice to remember names.
- **Synch.** Synchronize your body language and voice with the other person's.

Introductions

Introductions are an important part of business. Handling them graciously is a hallmark of a polished professional.

- Whenever possible, stand up to greet someone. It's just another way of removing barriers between you.
- Keep your handshake firm, quick, and respectful.
- Bring people together by introducing them to one another. Be seen as an accomplished facilitator. Introduce the big star to the smaller star.

- Don't wait to be introduced. Find someone to introduce you or keep your eyes open for opportunities to introduce yourself.
- If it's appropriate, tell your introducer one or two things to mention to your introducee.

Find Common Ground

The quicker you can find things in common with the person or people you are connecting with, the faster rapport can be established.

- Use the free information technique and ask questions that spark the imagination. Be curious about others.

10
Get Them Talking

Benjamin Disraeli became a member of the Parliament of Great Britain at thirty-three, and its prime minister at sixty-four. Disraeli's main political rival was William Gladstone, a four-time Liberal prime minister who was renowned for his abilities as a speaker.

One evening, Mr. Gladstone took a young woman out to dinner; the following evening, the same woman had dinner with Mr. Disraeli. Asked later what impressions the two distinguished men had made upon her, she replied, "After dining with Mr. Gladstone, I thought he was the cleverest person in England. After dining with Mr. Disraeli, I thought *I* was the cleverest person in England." Two eloquent, intelligent men—two completely different results. Judging by what we know of their reputations, Mr. Gladstone may have spent more time focusing the conversational spotlight on himself than on his guest, while Mr. Disraeli did the exact opposite. Perhaps Mr. Gladstone spent more time talking than his guest, while Mr. Disraeli made sure the opposite occurred. Mr. Disraeli had connected and built a relationship at a level much deeper and more memorable than a simple social or business contact.

Disraeli personified the three most charismatic really useful attitudes—*enthusiasm, curiosity,* and *humility*—while Gladstone overlooked the humility part. Have you ever watched a TV interview where the interviewer talks more than the guest? It's boring and annoying. The ground rules for successfully connecting are pretty much the same as they are for interviewing: Get the person talking, stay focused, actively observe, actively listen, give feedback and encouragement, and make sure you listen more than you talk. What better result could there be than to have your client walk away convinced that he or she is the most interesting person you ever met?

How to Get a Conversation Rolling

In organizations, conversation is the glue that holds everything together. CNN conducted a national poll that asked, "How good are you at business conversation?" There were three options to choose from. Of the 3,537 responses, 30 percent chose "I could carry on a great talk with a doorknob," 48 percent chose "I'm good sometimes, but it's mostly luck," and 22 percent chose "Uniformly terrible. I freeze, I stammer."

Ask yourself this question: Are my conversations like a game of tennis, where the action goes back and forth, or like a game of golf, where we may all be playing the same hole, but we get together only when it's time to write down the score? If you're tired of hitting the ball all by yourself, then look around. There are all kinds of people who are ready to teach you a little tennis.

I've been interviewed hundreds of times, and whenever I can, I ask my interviewers how they get people talking. It doesn't matter whether I'm talking to a print journalist, a radio personality, or a TV host. They all say the same thing: Questions are the spark plugs of conversation, especially open questions. Open questions get the ball rolling and open people up; closed questions shut them up. Open questions send you to the heart and emotions, while closed questions direct you to the head and logic. Any question that begins with "Who," "What," "Why," "Where," "When," or "How" calls for a visit to the imagination. Questions beginning with "Are you," "Did you," "Have you," request a logical, yes-or-no answer. For example:

Q: "Did you go to the store?"

A: "Yes."

Great, now I have to think of another question! Let's try it again with some questions that will start things rolling:

"Who was at the store?"

"What did you do on your way to the store?"

"Why did you go to the store?"

"Where is the store?"

"How did you get to the store?"

Every one of these questions requires the other person to go into their memory and play back their experience. The more sensory, rich, or imaginative the explanation, the more interesting the person appears and the better the conversation (and the connection) will be. And by asking the question and then drawing sensory detail out of the person you're talking with, you, like Disraeli, can make your companion feel like the cleverest person in the world.

In reality, you can't just come out like a customs officer and ask one blunt question after another. You must use a softer approach. You'll recall that when I was connecting with strangers in the streets, I softened my initial

EXERCISE

Questions Only

Have a conversation with a friend using only questions; in other words, you must answer a question with a question. This is a terrific way to hone your conversation skills.

On another day, whenever you are asked a question, answer it with a question. If you blow it, don't worry; no one will know.

approach with "Can I ask you a question?" Another easy way to do this in your day-to-day dealings is by coming up with a common-ground statement about the location or occasion to

Ask people questions that spark their imagination and ignite conversation.

prime the pump: "Looks like there are more exhibitors here than last year. How far have you come?" "Given the state of the road repairs around the store, how did you find the trip?" "It looks to me like everyone's talking and enjoying themselves. What do you think about holding these get-togethers more often?"

Another way to get a conversation rolling is by using direct commands to the imagination: "Tell me about . . ." You fill in the blank: "Tell me about your trip." "Tell me about those new guys on the fourth floor."

When you ask for an opinion or ask to be told something, you put the ball in the other person's court (to return to the tennis metaphor). When they send it back, watch out for *pointers* and choose the one that seems the most obvious. Pointers are words you can pick up and repeat back to your conversational partner as you steer and focus the conversation. I've italicized a few in the following lines from a recent conversation with the CFO of a midsized corporation.

"Tell me about your company's return policy," I said.

"For starters, we were forced to change our warehouse *procedures* last July because the *freight company* we deal with instituted new weight *restrictions.*" He sighed and shook his head. "It caused all sorts of *headaches* for the *shipping guys.*"

"How did the shipping guys respond to all the changes?"

That opened up the conversation. For the next few minutes I heard about personnel issues, problem-solving strategies, and a dozen ways things can go wrong. I kept the ball in play with a few questions, an attentive attitude, and feedback: a few head nods, a "yes" or two, and a shrug at one point. We went on for a while after that, and I will say that I learned a great deal. I can also say that the CFO walked away pretty sure that he was the most interesting man in the room.

Avoid questions that have simple yes-or-no answers.

But what can you do when you're pretty sure that you're the least interesting person in the room? Let me tell you about my friend George.

George, a human resources manager for one of the country's largest consulting companies, is over forty and a little self-conscious about it. He's been having trouble getting a conversation going with the junior staff, and he knows that if he wants to continue to be successful, he had better connect. One of his friends told him about the technique of answering a question with a question to break through with people you don't have that much in common with.

George has called an informal session with two of his staffers to figure out where to hold the company's next retreat.

"We should keep it nearer to town this year, George, don't you reckon?" said Dale, a self-important-looking twenty-five-year-old.

"How about the Lancaster?" asked George. The Lancaster had recently been transformed from a jaded old downtown flophouse into a snazzy boutique hotel.

"It's all right, but do you think it can handle three hundred and fifty?" said Jackie, who lives right around the corner from the Lancaster and would be much happier with three days at a country retreat.

"What's the best way to find out?" George replied.

"We can go by to check it out," Dale suggested.

"Any thoughts about doing it in September again?" George asked.

"September is all about being in the country," said Jackie. "What about going to the Boulders? It'll be just like the good old days."

"Aren't you a bit young to remember anything about the good old days?" Dale said sarcastically.

"I just thought that the idea was for people to have some fun as well," Jackie snapped.

"If we're looking for a good time, shouldn't we be talking about Las Vegas?" George asked, grinning. The other two looked at him, shocked for a moment, and then laughed. George joined them. *We're talking now, and I like it,* George thought. *We're a team, and I'm part of it.*

When George first heard about the technique of answering a question with a question in order to connect, he thought that it was a joke. Now that he's tried it, he thinks that it's genius. He's not only getting along with the younger staff now, but has picked up a couple of very nice ideas here as well.

The Art of Schmoozing

Somewhere in the first few minutes of your encounter, you'll feel the conversation start building a little momentum. Don't look for it; you'll know it when you feel it. Now is the time to move from polite and enquiring talk to something a little more personal. This requires a shift in attitude and intention. There's a qualitative distinction that we have to draw here between what I call *fact talk* and, for want of a better word, *schmoozing*. The fact talker appeals to a person's logical and analytical aspects, while the schmoozer talks to the senses and to the imagination.

Use your body as well as your eyes and voice to show you're paying rapt attention.

A great schmoozer's conversation is intimate and cozy, even gossipy. The schmoozer uses the magic words "who," "what," "where," "why," "when," and "how" to elicit emotional responses, while the fact talker uses these words only to elicit information. The schmoozer plays to the senses and asks, "How do you feel about . . . ? How do you see . . . ? How does this sound . . . ?" He uses linguistic softeners and artfully vague language to draw out his conversational partner: "Help me understand how we can make this work." "What are your first impressions?" "Tell me again why you think we ought to build there." A great schmoozer's opening line should make the schmoozee go directly into his or her imagination. Schmoozers sometimes nod and sway ever so slightly and even use gentle humming sounds to captivate and encourage their partner to respond. And when they do, the connection between them and their partner grows stronger. Fact talkers, with their emphasis on information, inevitably end up in a conversational dead end, playing tennis on their own.

Staying Focused

A schmoozer's language may be artfully vague and her body language gentle, but never doubt that a good schmoozer is always focused on what she wants. Even though she may lead you all over the place, she always has her goal in mind. She's always working her *KFC*. For example, let me tell you about Abigail, CEO of a midsized, middle-American manufacturing company that hired me for some consulting work. Abigail invited me to observe at an informal staff meeting. These meetings were designed

EXERCISE

Staying Focused

Keep yourself on track during any new business encounter by repeatedly asking yourself, What do I want? Tell yourself precisely what your desired outcome is, and stay positive. Remember your *KFC* all the way to the end of the first ninety seconds and beyond.

Try this with a friend. One of you is A, the other is B. A asks B, "Tell me about your job." B's task is to get off the subject as quickly as possible. A's job is to recognize as early as possible when this happens, then to use one of B's own phrases to stop B and get her back on track. For example:

to be a casual catch-up on the month's accomplishments and plans for the future. Abigail knows how to get intimate fast, how to look and listen actively, and how to stay focused.

Abigail is in front of her management team, catching some softball questions from her managers. She's finding out a lot more from them about how they're going to handle the next year's challenges than they're finding out from her because of her talent at schmoozing her way under the surface. She's been observing and listening but hasn't lost sight of why they are there. She uses the

A: "Tell me about your job."

B: "I sell photographic equipment. Ever since I was a kid I used to stare off at distant landscapes and—"

A: "I find landscapes fascinating. What does your job involve?"

Try this for three minutes, then swap roles. Don't worry about being obvious. The point of the exercise is to learn to recognize when you or the person you are talking to is wandering too far off-topic. You've seen the result when TV interviewers let their guests or, worse, themselves ramble on for no good reason. Interest and impact are diminished, and the connection can be lost.

meeting's informality to catch Mike, the head of their shipping division, with his guard down.

"Mike, congrats to you, what a month. I'm looking forward to your report."

"Thanks," replies Mike. "You know, we've been so busy running all over the place getting orders out, we just didn't have the time to write an official report. Do you guys mind if I just wing it?"

Even if the setting is informal, stay focused on getting the information you want.

Abigail smiles and bobs her head thoughtfully. Then she replies with a gentle tone. "Actually, I do mind, for two reasons. One, if your people are that stretched, they may be feeling up, or down, or close to rebellion. A written report would go a long way toward telling us how staff morale is holding up under all this pressure, as well as provide some hard numbers on customer satisfaction. And second, it sounds like you could have done with some help down there, but we can't give you what you don't ask for. Do you think you could have a report ready by our next meeting?"

Abigail knows that what she wants from this meeting is an in-depth and comprehensive look at where her company is at this very moment in time—and anyone who stands between her and that information, like Mike, had better watch out.

Schmoozing the Media

There are times when we all want to harness the power of the media (and other times when we want to squelch it, though hopefully fewer of those). You might have a great product or service about which you simply want to get the word out. But how can you do this? You need a real story—something that is newsworthy or interesting and sells papers, or attracts viewers and listeners. No journalist, editor, or host wants to be a billboard for you or your products.

One of the easiest ways to get your story out is by linking an aspect of your product or service directly to the good of the community. For example, one of the world's largest soft drink manufacturers is using its delivery systems in certain parts of the world to bring medicines to the out-of-the-way communities it services. This is interesting, and it gets ink and airtime.

If you can afford professional media training, get it—it's worth every penny. If you can't afford it, here are a few tips on connecting with the media. When it comes to the message, you should inform instead of sell. When it comes to the messenger, though, the three key aspects of convincing must be in place: credentials, logic, and emotion. Keep your message simple. Have one central point surrounded by four secondary points, and repeat them

Pay Attention—It's That Simple

In conversation, it's crucial to give physical and spoken feedback to maintain the connection. Show that you understand and are interested using your body language as well as your voice. The classic poor schmoozer is the person who never looks you in the eye—who's always looking over your shoulder at parties, hoping for a bigger, better score, a more important person to talk to. And they always get caught and resented. Look at, listen to, and focus on the one you're with. Fostering and maintaining a sense of closeness instills feelings of importance.

Stay curious. You'll find out what turns people on and what makes them tick by asking questions, by staying engaged, by drawing out your partner. What are their dreams? Now? As a child? What keeps them awake at night? How much would it help you to know what keeps your boss awake at night, or which of your coworkers are ambitious and which are content?

over and over. Come up with snappy, easy-to-understand sound bites that make sense and move people.

On a more grassroots level, consider the story of Penny Hill, who runs a Brooklyn, New York, nonprofit elder care program. She has more than two hundred elderly clients scattered throughout her neighborhood whom she and her volunteers feed and assist every day. One day, while she was walking past an office building, she saw a dumpster full of old computers. She thought nothing of it. When she got home, she sat down in the family room and idly watched her teenager at the family computer sifting through a screenful of e-mail.

Link your product or service to the good of the community.

Penny had an epiphany. "It was like a light went on over my head. I realized that for my daughter, e-mail, Facebook, and the Internet as a whole were important pipelines to her friends and to the world. Why couldn't they be the same for my elderly clients—most of whom had never used a computer? If they could learn to use them, these technologies could dramatically change their lives by putting them back in touch with the world. And they didn't need the newest or the fastest computer around. I could change their lives if only I could get some of those corporate computers before they landed in a dumpster."

Penny really had no clue how to get started. The first two corporations she got in touch with said they'd really love to help, but they had security and liability concerns about releasing their used computers. And all of her media contacts told her that they couldn't run a story about her wanting computers or trying to start a program. That was what advertising was for—come back when you have a story to tell. That was when Penny got a phone call that changed everything. One of her volunteers had

The Business Card—Treat It with Respect

We can learn a lot from Japanese business card rituals. The first thing that Japanese businessmen do is exchange cards, and the key to what follows can be summed up in one word: respect. Accept the card as if it were a gift—which it is. Hold it with both hands and take a moment to study what's written on it. If you can, respond to the card with an interested comment or an observation about something on the card—the person's title, credentials, location. What you have to understand is that a business card isn't just someone's name on a piece of paper; it's their corporate identity. Treat it with the respect the person deserves.

the two things that Penny needed most: a computer she was getting rid of and a teenage daughter who could teach one of Penny's clients how to use it. Now Penny had a big idea—to run an intergenerational experience exchange. The elderly get computer lessons, the teenagers get school credit for community service experience.

Within a few weeks, the recipient of that computer,

I've attended more corporate functions and more business conferences than I can remember. And over and over again, I see men and women taking someone's business card, flipping it over with barely a glance at what it says, and begin taking notes on the back. Never write on someone's business card in front of them. If you feel you absolutely have to note something from your conversation and you don't have a pad, ask them if they mind. It's good manners, and they'll appreciate the gesture.

When all this ceremony is done, put the card away in a top pocket, your purse, or your wallet—somewhere that shows respect. Never put the card in your back pocket, where it will get sat on.

Gil Gerard, an eighty-two-year-old patent attorney, was e-mailing his daughters in France, San Francisco, and Prague; was looking up some of his old protégés on the Internet; and had even given a couple of inventors some patent advice on an inventors' website. Now Penny had her story, so she took her big idea and hit every journalist she could find with her ten-second commercial: "Teenage tech support for surfing seniors."

She used the story of Gil and his teenage teacher to show what her program was doing for the community—both young and old. She wasn't trying to sell anything. She didn't say that she needed computers or volunteers, but she did show all three of the key aspects of convincing: credentials, logic, and emotion. And soon she had more computers, teenage teachers, and corporate donors than she knew what to do with.

Staying "Top of Mind"

Businesses spend billions on advertising, public relations, and publicity each year to keep themselves and their products at the forefront of public awareness. If you don't have billions, take heart. There's plenty you can do to keep yourself alive in your clients' mind—after all, what's the point of making a great first impression, establishing rapport, and getting your ideas across, if clients don't remember you when they are making decisions? It's not that they want to forget about you, it's just that most people lead very busy lives.

Being the right person, in the right place, at the right time has much more to do with being front and center in someone's memory than it has to do with luck. If you let your connections pass the ninety-day mark without renewing them, it's virtually certain that you will be unconsciously filed as "history." But if you keep your connections alive with legitimate, useful, and mutually beneficial contact, you will stay top of mind. It's up to you to keep in touch, let your clients know what you have to offer, and how you can make their lives easier.

In 2008 I spoke to several thousand Realtors at an event in San Diego. As part of my briefing, I was told that many agents didn't invest much time in after-sales. According to polling, 75 percent of home buyers and sellers were satisfied with their Realtor and said they would use the same agent again. Reality reflected that only 15 percent of them actually do.

The night before the event, I met with the industry's top salesperson for international sales—a successful person by anyone's standards. After a little playful prying on my part, he shared one of his secrets.

"So, what makes you different from the others?" I asked.

"Nothing really," he replied, "I work hard and do my homework."

Then his eyes twinkled. "Well," he said with a grin, "there is one thing."

Gifts aren't the only way to reach out to clients. Send an interesting Web link or make a useful inroduction to a person or service.

I raised my eyebrows. "What's that?"

I waited while he sipped at his glass of red wine.

"I have an account at Tiffany."

Intrigued, I asked him to tell me more.

"A couple of weeks after clients move into their new home, they receive a small package via FedEx. Inside is a silver key engraved with their names, their new address, and the date they made the purchase. Enclosed alongside the beautiful Tiffany box is a simple thank-you card from me. There is no mention of my name or anything to do with business anywhere, except on the card."

What a classy thing to do! The new owners will tell the story of how they received the gift, and the Realtor stays alive in their minds. Not only has he attached himself to a world-class brand, but this simple gift is out there, like a foot soldier, working away on his behalf.

Not everyone can afford to shop at Tiffany—and even if you can, a gift like this may not be appropriate in your business—but there are plenty of other ways to stay top of mind. You can e-mail a Web link or send a magazine clipping that you think a client would find interesting or that would further the client's professional development. You could introduce two clients with mutual interests over lunch. You could connect your client with a new resource, such as a caterer, a photographer, or an architect. You can bake cookies and drop them off at the client's office during the holidays. (Sound corny? Forget it. A very successful financial planner I know, who is also a brilliant baker, brings fresh cookies to some of her clients. They are always *very* happy to see her.) If you aren't a baker, figure out another strategy. Use your imagination and a little *KFC* (see page 31)!

90-Second Summary

How to Get Them Talking

The ground rules for successfully connecting are:
Get them talking, and keep them talking. Stay focused, actively observe, actively listen, give feedback and encouragement, and make sure to listen more than talk.

Questions

Questions are the spark plugs of conversation. Asking

the right kind of questions helps keep the conversational ball rolling.

- Ask open questions, which open people up and send them to their heart and imagination. They can't be answered with a simple "yes" or "no," and they often begin with "who," "what," "where," "why," "when," or "how."
- Avoid closed questions, which shut people down. They can often be answered with a single word, and they sometimes begin with "Are you?" "Did you?" "Have you?"
- Use direct commands to the imagination: "What do you think about . . . ?" "Tell me about . . . "
- Actively listen for pointers to pick up and repeat back as questions to your conversational partner.
- Try answering a question with a question—it can help create a sense of rapport.

Schmoozing

When conversation builds momentum, it's time to move from polite and inquiring talk to something a little more personal.

- The schmoozer's language appeals to the senses and to the imagination, while the fact talker asks merely for information. A great schmoozer's conversation is intimate and cozy, even gossipy.
- Schmoozers know the value of building relationships and that the best way you can approach anyone is to be introduced by someone he or she respects.
- Stay focused on your goals and keep yourself on track throughout the conversation. Remind yourself of the desired outcome and stay positive.
- It's crucial to give physical and verbal feedback. Show with your body language that you understand and are interested in the other person.
- Focus on the person you're with. That sense of closeness between you will instill feelings of importance in your partner.
- Stay curious. By asking questions, staying engaged, and drawing out your partner, you will find out what makes him tick.
- If you're offered a person's business card, treat it with respect.

Schmoozing the Media

Inform; don't sell. Link an aspect of your big idea and your ten-second commercial directly to the good of the community.

Staying Top of Mind

Make an effort to reach out to clients and potential clients on a regular basis. Tailor your outreach to their interests and needs. You can send an interesting clipping or Web link, or introduce them to a potential customer. Or you can just drop off some treats.

11 Find the Right Approach

We've spent a lot of time so far learning how to verbally and nonverbally make meaningful connections with other people. We've also looked at how to artfully craft ideas and objectives into convincing messages. Now it's time to consider the actual route you will use to deliver these messages. It's all very well and good to make people feel trusting and receptive toward you and your ideas, but if you don't deliver them with the right approach, it can all be a terrific waste of time and opportunity.

There are many ways you can eat noodles—with a fork, with chopsticks, or with your fingers, to name but three. There are many ways to deliver good news—by fax, by skywriting, or in person. And there are many ways to find a job—through the want ads, on the Internet, or by building networks. The number of approaches is as large as your imagination will allow. In the story of Abigail's staff meeting, in the last chapter, she could have chosen a more formal appproach to get a good look at her company, but she chose a less formal approach to get what she wanted. The trick is to know how to read the situation so that you choose the right tack.

Part of choosing the right tack is knowing the state of mind of the person or group you're with. We've referred many times throughout this book to the power of adjusting your attitude. But when connecting with others, the difference between success and failure can rest in your ability to adjust *their* attitude or, to be more precise, to adjust their emotional state of mind.

Structure the Emotional Context of Your Encounter

Let's say you have an idea about how to streamline and improve the way your office shares production information, and you want to persuade your boss to adopt the system. The question is how to get your overworked, harried boss excited about it. Sometimes getting people to move from one emotional state to an entirely different one can be difficult. For example, if you intend to move someone from indifference ("I'm busy; I've got a lot of other things on my mind; can't this wait?") to excitement ("Great idea—let's do it!") in one fell swoop, you may be in for a challenge.

Years ago, Drs. Richard Bandler and John Grinder, the geniuses behind Neuro-Linguistic Programming, identified the behavioral processes used by highly persuasive individuals. That is, they not only figured out *what* these persuaders do, they also figured out *how* they do it. They discovered that persuasively gifted people, wittingly or unwittingly, link three or four emotional states together in order to arrive at their desired outcome. In other words, instead of going directly from state A (indifference) to state D (enthusiasm), they lead you from A through states B and C to D. So rather than attempting a direct shift in state from indifference to enthusiasm, an experienced persuader might move you from indifference to curiosity, then to openness, before arousing your enthusiasm. This is called *linking states,* and it's a powerful way to get people emotionally connected with you and/or your ideas.

Once you've decided on the states of mind to be employed, the next thing you, as a gifted persuader, would do is to get yourself into the first link on the chain. You won't be convincing if you're not congruent. The simple act of adjusting yourself into a state of curiosity will make your body language, tone of voice, and choice of words rub off on the other. Practice rotating through the feelings of curiosity, openness, and enthusiasm over and over: ten seconds each will do. This is why I had you bouncing around the office like a kangaroo and a cougar, a winner and a loser in earlier exercises. It was to give you the discipline and flexibility of attitude and behavior necessary to lead and link emotions—not just in yourself, but in others.

Now for the words you use: Even if they constitute only 7 percent of your total message, they must be chosen with care. You learned earlier the value of sensory-rich language, painting word pictures, and the power of the imagination. Now it's time to "Muldoonize" your conversation by including emotionally charged words. Adopting the emotional state yourself will help bring the right words to mind. To give you an idea of how someone might link states to get another person primed to hear her idea, let's listen in on Joanna. Joanna knows her boss, Max, commutes to work on the train, and she knows that a great way to start a conversation is with a question. Max is sitting at his desk.

"Max, did you come in on the train this morning?"

"Sure."

"Have you ever met the guy who drives the train? I haven't. But as I was riding in this morning, with the cars and the people and the buildings whizzing by, I thought how curious it is that every day thousands of people get up and place their lives in the hands of complete strangers. We do it all the time. We trust others to get us to work safely, to take care of our kids, to make meals for us . . .

But it's worth it, right? Trusting others opens up our lives to endless possibilities—trying new flavors in exotic restaurants, flying through the sky to a sun-drenched island, or riding a roller coaster with your family—you name it. There are always so many possibilities in everything, even here at work. And listen, what I came in to talk to you about is this possibility. If we hire some bright kids as interns to help with the grunt work, it will free up the assistants to do more substantive stuff, which will allow the rest of us to spend more time generating new business. Just imagine, six months from now when . . . "

You are reading only the words here, devoid of body language, facial expression, voice tone, volume, and inflection—devoid of emotional state. Nevertheless, you can imagine that once Joanna got herself in the mood, it was easy to deliver this speech in a genuine, heartfelt way and have its emotional effects rub off on her boss. She moved convincingly from state to state and offered a cause-and-effect benefit, just before linking the whole thing to the future with "Just imagine, six months from now when . . . "—a sure way to engage her boss's imagination and get him involved. And all this took only ninety seconds or less. This is the secret of great communicators.

Find an opportunity to listen to a speech that moved a nation, by a great communicator such as Martin Luther King Jr., Winston Churchill, Eleanor Roosevelt, Franklin

D. Roosevelt, John F. Kennedy, or Nelson Mandela, and identify the states they led their audiences through before rousing them to action. When Churchill looked grand, you could feel it yourself, and when he acted angry, you could feel that, too. When Martin Luther King Jr. said, "I've been to the mountaintop," your spirit was uplifted with him.

The next time you want to get someone excited about an idea, figure out ahead of time which three or four emotional states make sense to link together to get the person—whether it's a client, interviewer, boss, team,

EXERCISE

Linking States

Here's a charades-like exercise to help you practice adjusting other people's emotional states. It's best done in a group of three or four.

On separate pieces of paper, have each person write three states of mind they want to rouse in the others. These could include curious, excited, sad, confused, joyful, confident, free, secure, adventurous, sexy, lonely—whatever you like. Fold them, put them in a bowl, and mix them up.

Pick a state from the bowl and, without saying what's written on the piece of paper, attempt, in thirty seconds or less, to elicit that state in the others. You can use stories, metaphors, body language, and voice tone, but you or audience—excited about you and/or your ideas. Your desired outcome must be a win-win situation or you'll encounter resistance. Joanna began her conversation with her boss with a question and a couple of "verifiables." These are questions or statements that her boss knew to be true: Yes, he came in on the train, and no, he doesn't know the driver. Verifiables have the double effect of engaging the person, or persons, and getting immediate agreement.

You can practice linking states in any of your daily activities—in dating, during meetings, socializing, ordering

can't name the state. For example, say you picked "curious." You might say "You won't believe what I saw around the corner as I was pulling in here today. I parked as fast as I could and ran back to the corner but it was gone. Then I saw it again, but this time it was . . ." At the end of thirty seconds the others have to tell what they were feeling. If they all don't say "curious," ask them to show you how they'd interpret that state.

After everybody has a turn, the group repeats the exercise, but this time each person picks two states and tries to make the other players first feel one way, then another in sixty seconds or less. Then try linking three emotional states in ninety seconds or less.

a pizza, borrowing a library book. It may sound like an odd, unnatural thing to do, but it is simpler than you think. To a certain degree, you already do it; you'll just be enhancing your natural abilities. It won't take long before linking states becomes second nature and even part of your explanatory style. How you use this technique is up to you, your comfort level, and your imagination. What I'm giving you is the structure behind this persuasive approach.

Now let's look at some of the nuts and bolts of everyday business situations, from trying to land a job, to working the phones, to maximizing the potential in social situations. Always keep what you've learned about linking emotional states at the back of your mind, because it will help you get what you want in just about any circumstance.

Getting Job Interviews

Say you're ready to make a move from your current work. How do you approach finding your next job? According to MSNBC, job seekers who use the want ads are successful only 5 percent of the time, while the success rate jumps to two-thirds for those who invest their time in networking. *The Wall Street Journal* reported that more than 90 percent of people get new business and jobs by networking. Hiring managers also overwhelmingly prefer networking for recruiting new employees. In one study, almost half revealed they fill up to 25 percent of their openings before ever publicly advertising them, preferring to network within their companies as well as outside before resorting to the assistance of a search firm or a paid advertisement.

How can you make this work in your favor? Try following the example of my old friend Alfred. Alfred lost his job as vice president of a savings and loan company when it was sold. What he didn't lose was his talent for making connections—and knowing what to do with them. Within three weeks he had gathered the names of 134 people who might be able to help him in his job search; he had met with thirty-seven of them and received three job offers. And it all happened because he knew how to network.

Alfred's plan had two steps. First, he tried to have a face-to-face meeting with whomever he could; second, he got two referrals from everyone he met with. Starting with his own contacts, he phoned and said, "I want to talk to you about something. I am looking for a job. I'm not calling to ask you for a job, but rather two names of people I can contact. As you know, I have . . . [here he lets slip his ten-second commercial, plus his credentials]. I'd like to be able to use your name as an introduction, not a reference. That's all I want."

When he called the people he was referred to, he said, "I'll do breakfast, lunch, dinner, coffee at midnight—whatever it takes to meet you face-to-face." The purpose of the call was to get them to say, "Yes, I'll meet you."

What Alfred was doing was getting himself out there. The call and the meetings were opportunities to showcase himself. There was little pressure to give him a job because all he asked for was referrals. Within five years, Alfred had made more than a comeback—he was chairman of a major national mortgage bank. And he's still making new connections.

Job Interviews

An interview is a presentation with you as the subject. As in any presentation, you need a hook and a point, an opening and a close (for more on this, see Chapter 12). And like any presenter, you need to learn how to breathe; we'll talk about this in Chapter 13. For now, let's talk about your hook.

Remember your ten-second commercial? Well, just like a smart advertiser, sometimes you want to hit a very specific audience. Advertisers look at demographic slices—say, women eighteen to thirty-four. You're looking to score with a nine-to-five audience. That's a slightly silly way of saying you should customize your ten-second commercial before you walk into an interview.

Don't just do your homework. Put what you learn to work.

Do your homework. Learn all you can about the company (and the interviewer, too, if possible). Get a copy of any sales literature and the firm's annual report. Type the company's name into a search engine and see how far you can go. Research it in online business archives and information services (even if it costs you a buck or two, it's worth it). Call anyone you know who does business with the company or, even better, works there. If all else fails, talk to the receptionist when you arrive.

The old adage "Information is strength" drives me nuts because it's not true. Information is potential strength; it's not worth much until you use it. Use your information to craft a ten-second commercial that ties you to the company—that shows how your experience, skills, and strengths make you the person they want for this job, and then give it the pub approach. But don't think that you can fake it. This has got to be real and you need to deliver it with emotion.

Follow Up

Always, always, always follow up your interview—it can be the deal clincher. Do it within twenty-four hours and aim to take thirty seconds of the person's time. You can send a note, an e-mail, or leave a phone message. My advice is to leave an after-hours voice message—it shows you don't want to interrupt the working day and that you are genuinely interested. Voice tone and word content are vital. Adjust your attitude before you make the call and make it standing up. Be enthusiastic and courteous. Say thank you for the interview, be enthusiastic about the position, and keep your ten-second commercial in mind as you reinforce some positive aspect of the interview. If you choose a written reply, make sure your grammar and spelling are perfect.

Whatever format you choose, customize your message, practice, and keep this important self-marketing sales tool as close to thirty seconds as you can.

Schmoozing in the Phone Zone

When you're on the phone, you may have a great connection, but you have to be sure that you're *making* a great connection. There's no body language for you to read. Your only clues to what your conversational partner is thinking or feeling are his words and tone of voice. That's all he has to read you, too. So you must be vigilant about both how you sound and how you're expressing yourself.

Remember that when you're feeling anxious, the tension can come through in your voice and make the other person feel the same way. If you care about the person on the other end of the phone, adjust your attitude before you make the call.

Let's listen in to a phone call between Dennis and Bill, from different departments in the same corporation. They barely know each other, but this phone call could change all that.

"Listen, Bill, this is Dennis Evans from advanced applications." Dennis's voice sounds tight and his words come racing out of the receiver.

"Right. Got it." Bill speaks deliberately, hoping Dennis will pick up on the cue.

"I don't know why I'm doing this—everyone else is on vacation and that's where I should be, too. Anyway, we came up with this idea for monetizing our site by selling ring tones, and we've found the guy who can do it for us, and all we need is for you guys in the legal department to get the agreement with him done. I have to give Christine in sales some assurances that this thing is going to happen so she can present it to the president, so we need it tomorrow." Dennis hasn't breathed yet, much less slowed down. If anything, he sounds like he's winding up a little tighter.

"Are you kidding? You're just telling me about this now? Do you have any idea how much we've got to get

On the phone, your tone and pacing are just as important as the words you choose.

out before Christmas? This will need due diligence and . . ." Bill knows he shouldn't respond in kind, but he can't help having some of his frustration come out in his voice.

"I'm so tired of excuses," Dennis bellows. "We're under pressure to get things done, and all I hear is reasons why they can't be. You can't do this but you can do that crappy deal with the Dutch that leaves us with huge liabilities. You can rush to do something lousy but you take your time to do something good." Dennis doesn't wait for an answer. He slams down the phone as soon as the last word comes out of his mouth.

Bill, one ear aching, wishes that he'd never picked up the phone.

Sound familiar? It didn't have to be that way. If Dennis had taken a few deep breaths before picking up the receiver, he might have chosen a more fruitful approach. Because Bill could not see Dennis, Bill's imagination was available for stimulation. This is the time for metaphor and sensory-rich language. Here's how this phone call could have gone:

"Hi, Bill, this is Dennis Evans, upstairs. It's time for the dreamers and the doers to get together."

"What's up?"

"Just a little Christmas present for Christine Burgin, who heads up sales."

"Oh yes?"

"And I just need your help to wrap it up."

"Shoot."

In the first example, Dennis lost sight of what he wanted; he was more interested in venting than communicating. In the second, he juiced up the conversation with metaphors: dreamers instead of advanced applications, doers instead of the contracts department, Christmas present instead of agreement. Smooth, pleasant, and effective: A good phone schmoozer does not waste other people's time but, by the same token, does not rush things. Now there's a chance that the job may get finished.

Cold Calls

Just about the toughest ninety seconds in business are the first minute and a half of a cold call, but they can be necessary. Muldoon once told me that people who make three times more phone calls than their competitors are four times more successful.

Today's well-trained salespeople know the value of building relationships through networking, customer retention, community and business group involvement,

EXERCISE

Sleight of Head

How would you like to be able to influence the outcome of closed questions—those "Did you?" and "Have you?" and "Are you?" questions. Here's a little something I teach to frontline service personnel. You can adapt this to work for you in almost any situation. It's a way of sending out the answer you want with the question. It works in many situations because of congruity and synchrony—two instinctive aspects of human behavior I've referred to many times in these pages.

You're on a flight. The flight attendants are moving through the plane, clearing up after a snack has been served. Time is tight. How do the attendants keep you from asking for another cup of coffee or glass of wine even as they say, "Can I get you anything else?" They almost imperceptibly shake their heads "no" when asking the question. Try it yourself: Ask "Do you want to schedule a follow-up meeting?" while gently shaking your head "no." There is a very strong probability the answer will be in the negative. If you nod an almost imperceptible "yes," the chances are high they will say "Yes."

referrals from satisfied customers, public speaking, and becoming a prominent authority. But they also know that if you want to grow your sales, you need new customers.

And getting new customers means making new connections. Wendy Kohler, founder of TalentedWomen.com, put together a TV talk show series; signed up eight major sponsors and a roster of high-profile guests from the media, government, and industry; and got a TV station to write up a juicy contract—all through cold calling. How did she manage it when all but one of her contacts were complete strangers? Like many sales reps, she did something like what Alfred did. She turned down the heat. Her first calls were for referrals; she didn't try to sell right away. And these calls and requests for referrals gave her the opportunity to showcase her idea, deliver her ten-second commercial and her credentials, and spread the word without the pressure of the person having to buy. By the time she started calling potential sponsors and guests, she had strong introductions and had built some good buzz about her project. By the time she was serious about getting people to sign on the dotted line, people wanted in—they didn't have to be sold. The connection was there before she even called.

This technique works just as well around the office. Trying to initiate a project? Talk to your coworkers about who might be able to help you advance it. Who might benefit from it being a success? Turn down the heat a little and you may find that people who can help you may be a lot more willing to come on board.

Socializing

Business-related social functions are about meeting people and making connections, not about eating well or having a ball. You should prepare for them like an athlete getting ready for a competition. Following are some things to keep in mind.

Know What You Want

Seasoned socializers know why they are attending an event long before they set foot in the place. Whether it's to check out the competition or to find out who may be restless, who's hot, or who's hiring, you've got to know what you want from the evening and set specific goals.

Adjust Your Attitude, or Go Home

Remember your attitude precedes you. You make a statement long before you open your mouth, so be sure to walk into the room with a really useful attitude. Make direct eye contact and smile.

Get Yourself Introduced

The best way you can approach anyone is to be introduced by someone he or she respects. Make it a habit to introduce others and the favor will be returned. If you don't know anyone, introduce yourself. It's perfectly fine, and expected, to walk straight up to a stranger, look them in the eye, smile, open your body language, put out your hand, and introduce yourself. "Hello, I'm Anna Osborne from the Cigna Group. What do you think of the conference so far?" Be sure to have your business cards and your ten-second commercial at the ready. Some folks even include the commercial, *discreetly,* on their cards.

Stay Focused

Stay focused on greeting and meeting people and on getting into conversations. Make eye contact, find common ground. The bar and the hors d'oeuvres table are for others—not for you. Focus on the person you are talking with—scan the room for a more important prospect at your immediate peril. If you do spot someone you want or need to talk with, close your conversation and gracefully excuse yourself before moving on to another person or group. Manners do count.

Join a Group

If there's someone you really want or need to talk to and they're already in a conversation, listen before jumping in. Make eye contact with the person you want to talk to, smile, and listen until he or she includes you. Introduce yourself when there is a pause in the conversation. If you feel an overwhelming urge to add something relevant to a conversation and you don't get a verbal or nonverbal invitation to join in, take the plunge, but make sure you introduce yourself soon afterward with a smile and eye contact.

Let's Do Lunch

All over the world, more business is carried out in restaurants, bistros, and cafés than in offices, factories, or the backs of trucks. Breaking bread together on neutral ground is a terrific way to evaluate people, strengthen relationships, and, sure, sometimes discuss business. Of course, that's the upside. It's also a brilliant venue to showcase your lack of manners, your questionable conversation skills, and your ability to stay focused and be gracious at the same time.

Business lunches are all about establishing rapport. Begin hunting for common ground even before you meet. A few days before your lunch, start skimming a newspaper and the Internet for news that relates to the other person's business. If there's no news about her business, pay attention to the stories of the day; they are instant common ground (but stay away from politics).

If you take clients out on a regular basis, it's worth developing a relationship with a few choice restaurants, say an upscale bistro, a posh pub, and a high-end café—or whatever feels right for you and your wallet. Make sure the places you choose have the right atmosphere for business. Besides cleanliness, reputation, and accessibility, bear in mind three things: Does it look good? Is it comfortable? Can we talk without shouting (or being overheard)? Get to know the staff. You invested time and money learning your business and honing your skills. Now go out and invest a little in getting to know the manager, the maître d', and the waiters—these folks can be the tools of your trade as much as your briefcase and your BlackBerry.

On the Golf Course

Thomas sells financial products. In fact, he does it very well, but some of Thomas's coworkers wonder how he has both great sales numbers and a year-round tan. "Sometimes I've just got to get out of the office to get *any* business done," says Thomas, laughing. He calls his golf games the four-hour sales call, but when pushed a little further, he admits they're really just a great way to build relationships and have some quality time with his clients.

A game of golf is a chance for four hours of uninterrupted information gathering and connection building that you could never accomplish in an office, where the phones are ringing and a crisis walks in the door every time you start to get to the good stuff. I followed Thomas out to a driving range, where we had this conversation in between working on our short irons.

"I use the first six holes to connect and get the conversation rolling," Thomas says. "I use polite, inquisitive small talk to get to know all about my customers, their families, interests, and backgrounds." He drops a gorgeous iron shot on the practice green and smiles as it backs up to the hole. "I gently look for things we have in common and when I find them, I know that the relationship is going to warm up.

"I use the next six holes to learn about the nature of their business and find areas of common purpose." He pauses to pull a driver out of his bag. "I've noticed the attitude and physicality of the game change when we talk like this. Some people become more aggressive, others more relaxed." Boom. That drive must have been close to 250 yards, straight down the middle. Thomas grins over at me as he continues. "We use the last six holes to talk about their most pressing needs and what my company and I can do to help them. I never pull out an order form or start talking deal points out on the course, but you better believe that I'm his first call the next morning."

As he tosses his driver back into his golf bag, Thomas says, "The secret out here and in business is that once you've made the shot, you've got to have a great follow-through."

There are a lot of factors that impact your success at connecting in business. Making a good first impression, appearing happy and confident, demonstrating a sense of curiosity, and showing flexibility are paramount. These are easier to achieve if you are confident in your ability to manage and direct others' chain of emotions. Linking emotional states will not only make you and your ideas more appealing and more memorable, it will also give you strength, commitment, and focus. Enjoy the process, improve with practice, and watch as your confidence level rises.

90-Second Summary

Finding the Right Approach

- **Linking states.** You can influence the attitude with which you and your ideas are received. Figure out which emotional states to link together to take people from where they are now to where you want them to be. Using your own attitude, sensory-rich language, and body language, practice linking emotional states at home, at work, at play. Practice, practice, practice!

- **Job interviews.** Research the company before your interview. Use the information you glean to craft a convincing ten-second commercial that connects you with the company—one that shows how your experience, skills, and strengths make you the ideal person for the job.

- **On the phone.** There's no body language for you to read on the phone, no clue to what your conversational partner is thinking or feeling except for his words and tone of voice. Likewise, he has no way to know what you're thinking or feeling. So you must be vigilant about how you sound and how you express yourself. Your tone and pacing are just as important as the words you choose.
- **Socializing.** A business lunch or other social occasion is about connecting, exploring, and sharing. To socialize most effectively, remember to know what you want, have a useful attitude and open body language, get yourself introduced, stay focused on making connections, and join a group if you need to.

12

The Secrets of the Great Communicators

My introduction to the art of making presentations came, naturally enough, from Francis Xavier Muldoon in the late 1960s at the Savoy, London's finest luxury hotel. One November afternoon I followed him down a Persian-carpeted hallway to a meeting room.

"Two hundred seats?" Muldoon asked the bellman as we entered.

"Right, sir. Theater, no podium," the bellman answered, and Muldoon peeled off a ten-shilling note.

"Thank you, Peter."

"But Frank," I said as Peter walked away, "Don't you want me to organize more chairs?"

"Why would that be?" Muldoon replied, walking toward the stage.

"We've got two hundred and thirty-three confirmations."

I should have known better. Muldoon didn't make mistakes.

"Nicko," he said, with that twinkle in his eye. "Most companies will book a room with 500 seats when they have 450 people registered for an event. Sixty don't show and the room's half empty. If I speak to 450 people, I'll book a room with 350 seats, hold a few chairs in reserve, and have the place packed. Standing room only creates an atmosphere of success. A half-empty room smells of failure. Do you get my point?"

I did.

These were the "swinging sixties" and London led the world in music, fashion, and art. Cream, the Rolling Stones, and the Beatles blasted from bootleg radio stations. Twiggy, the world's first supermodel, posed for *Vogue* on Carnaby Street in a Mary Quant outfit, while the members of *Monty Python's Flying Circus* paraded about as old women in overcoats and hair rollers, and James Bond suavely saved the world in his Aston Martin DB5. It was a glamorous and exciting time to be in advertising.

Half an hour later the room filled with advertising executives, analysts, media buyers, the sales staff from our own ad department at *Woman* magazine, and some of the editorial staff. I counted eighteen people standing after much jostling for position. Lots of energy. Good buzz.

Muldoon stepped onstage and waited until the room fell quiet. Then, without so much as a "Hello" or a "Welcome" or a "Thanks for coming," he held up the most recent copy of the magazine.

Looking solemnly around the room, he deliberately tore off the back cover. Then he waved it aloft and declared slowly, "Anyone who would pay £7,500 for this is a raving lunatic!"

While his audience sat in stunned silence, he broke into a smile, slapped the torn-off page against the rest of the magazine, and pronounced, "But attach it to this, and you have the most powerful and cost-effective vehicle this country can offer you to deliver your message to four million avid and consuming women. And why is it so popular? Why do so many people read it and trust it? Because each and every issue is a must-have weekly fix of spicy celebrity news, juicy television insider gossip, and hearty real-life stories. It's the number one choice for up-to-the-minute lifestyle treats, fresh ideas on healthy family-friendly food, and spur-of-the-moment travel deals."

Time elapsed so far: thirty seconds. And Muldoon had this roomful of people riveted.

"We are less than five minutes away from Covent Garden," Muldoon continued, holding the copy of the magazine in his hand, "where freshness, variety, excellent value, expert knowledge, high standards, and . . . "

For the next two minutes he evoked wonderful images of the market, England's largest, as a foil for what he was really talking about—the magazine. He went on to describe how to take full advantage of the magazine's massive reach. Flipping carelessly through the open magazine, he said, "Four million people step inside every week not because they drifted in but because they make a conscious decision to do so. It's part of their routine."

Muldoon switched to direct comparisons. "*Woman* magazine is kind of like Covent Garden Market. The market, like the magazine, has sections for eating and drinking, culture, and entertainment that deliver measurable results for their business partners. It, like the magazine, has seasonal sections that continually drive new ideas and trends." He gave them circulation figures, readership profiles, and response rates, all the time linking to the parallel experience he had created in the mind of his audience—the nearby market. It wasn't overt but Muldoon knew his audience would link the magazine to all the evocative sensory images he created when they made their next advertising decisions.

After four and a half minutes he swung into his interactive close. I was stationed by the door, ready to do my part.

"Before you take your leave today . . . " That was my cue. I opened the doors at the left side of the stage and in marched four merchants from Covent Garden pushing two handcarts. All eyes went to the carts. "We want to present you all with a token of our gratitude for attending this afternoon." The audience applauded.

The carts were piled with white cardboard boxes the size of small briefcases. On the front of each one, the cover of the latest issue of *Woman*; on the back was a summary of his presentation, designed to evoke the flavor of the market; on the spine were advertiser testimonials; and inside the box was an assortment of fruit, cheeses, nuts, and of course, the latest issue of *Woman* in a clear plastic wrap. Muldoon was smart. He knew most people in the audience would be heading directly home after he finished his presentation and they'd peruse the package during their commute.

Capture Their Imagination and Capture Their Hearts

A little later we left the Savoy, crossed the Strand, and began the five-minute stroll back to the office. It was almost 5:00 in the evening when we passed the Nag's Head Pub, a famous hangout for newspaper, magazine, and advertising types at this time of day. My boss said, "Come on. It's too late to go back to the office now. Let's celebrate."

Make sure your audience, whether it's one person or 1,000, knows why they're listening to you.

The "Nag's" was noisy and bustling with writers, editors, advertising sales agents, artists, and the usual 24-hour crowd that accompany the print business. There was lots of laughter, clinking glasses, and boasting about the day's adventures. Muldoon shook a few hands and slapped some backs. From out of nowhere a pint of their best bitter appeared in my hand and we joined the bantering.

Muldoon nodded at an empty table over by the window. I led the way and pulled out a chair. "Okay. Feedback time." He sat down across from me, a glass of claret in his hand. "What did you notice? What did you see?" It sounded more like a song title than one of his debriefings.

"Lots." Where to begin? "You riveted them right off the top."

Muldoon raised his distinguished gray eyebrows and smiled.

"When you tore off the page and said 'Anyone who'd pay £7,500 for it would be a raving lunatic' they couldn't take their eyes off you. You really got their attention."

"Excellent." He sipped his claret.

"Your point was right there at the top, too: 'the most powerful and cost-effective vehicle this country can offer you to deliver your message to four million avid and consuming women.'"

"Well done. You remembered the golden rule: *No point? No presentation.* Nothing exasperates an audience more than not knowing what they are doing there. Your point must contain a cause and effect they can relate to. Do *X,* and this desired result happens. Don't do it, and *Y* happens. The point captures reason and logic. It means your presentation makes sense. Then all you have to do is prove your point.

"Before you can convince an audience of anything, you have to capture their attention. Capture their attention and you can capture their interest. Once you have their interest, you can fire up their imagination. And their heart will surely follow." He looked across at the waitress and nodded. "Capture the waitress's attention and the food will surely follow, too."

Shish Kebabs

I ordered fish-and-chips. Muldoon chose something called the "Espetada." The menu said it was "a typical Portuguese dish made of chunks of beef rubbed in garlic and salt, then barbecued, and served on a skewer that hangs from a hook on a stand." It was really just a fancy name for a shish kebab.

"Nicko, 80 percent of the time people have no clue why they do anything. They make their decisions based on their emotions—on what their hearts imagine they want—even though they think they're being rational. Once you can step inside someone's imagination with your words, you can set off a reaction that creates pictures, sounds, feelings, smells, and tastes. A sensory reaction that brings things alive and makes them real."

He pointed out the window across the street. "See that pathway leading to the tube station? A blind beggar used to sit there before they cleaned up this area. The old man had a sign in his lap with just two words written on it: "I'm Blind." Passersby would drop the odd bit of change into his cap from time to time but the pickings were slim. Then, on a sunny April morning, one of the junior advertising men from the office asked if he could add a few words to the man's sign. The blind man said sure; he recognized the young man's voice as someone who often dropped in a few coins and wished him luck. The adman turned the sign over and wrote five words on the back and placed it back in the blind man's lap. At the end of the day, the adman stopped by to see how things had been going. The blind man said he couldn't believe his ears when the coins came tumbling in. 'What did you write on my sign?' he asked. 'Not much. I just added three words,' the adman replied. 'Three words made so much difference?' 'Three words that fire up the imagination can.' The beggar insisted that the young man tell him what he'd written on the sign."

Muldoon took a long, slow sip of his claret. "Right. Where's that food?"

"Well? What did it say?"

"What did what say?"

"The sign."

"Oh that. Capture your interest, did I? With my little story."

I laughed.

The waitress arrived balancing the food. The fish-and-chips were golden and crispy. The Espetadas came with mash and onions—the pub grub touch.

Muldoon opened a linen napkin and tucked one corner into his collar. "Right. Tuck in."

"The sign, Frank?"

"Oh that. It said, 'It's spring. And I'm blind.'"

"Ha! Clever. It made people stop and think—imagine what it would be like to be the beggar," I said. "And it captured a few hearts."

"Exactly. And, more to the point, it captured wallets, too." Muldoon wiped his fingers on the napkin and sipped his claret. "All great communication comes down to a few catchy emotional words. They should hit four hot buttons." He tapped his finger on the table as he reeled them off. "Attention, interest, desire, and action."

(continued on page 254)

Recipe for a Shish Kebab

Shish kebab has just four ingredients: a hook, a point, some steak, and some sizzle.

The hook. Something to grab the attention of your audience from the get-go. Muldoon was prone to dramatic hooks like dumping envelopes onto the floor (see page 14), and tearing off the magazine's back cover, and using the word *lunatic.* But you could use a physical hook, like wearing a blindfold to demonstrate that an organization has lost its way, or pretending you can't pull your hands out of your pockets for thirty seconds to illustrate budget restraints. Another captivating way to open is by citing a provocative quotation, a stunning statistic, or a shocking headline.

The point. Your single brief message stated in the positive voice. "*The people who get ahead today are the ones who . . .*" not "*The people who don't get ahead are the ones who don't . . .*" The point should run through everything because your entire presentation must prove your point. Make sure your presentation answers the three questions, "So what?" "Who cares? and What's in it for me?"

Three chunks of steak and a little sizzle. In this context, steak is the hard data your listeners

need to know to be able to make a decision: costs, market conditions, competition, timing, support, sales, whatever is pertinent to deciding to move forward. Stick to three key points. The sizzle can be a prop (an umbrella, a cape, a golf club), an interaction, a humorous anecdote (but avoid jokes, because unless everyone gets the joke, you'll divide your audience), or audience involvement (asking someone to remember—or forget—a word or number, or anything that gets one or all of them to do or say something). Muldoon relied on theatrical delivery to impart sizzle. He would freeze in his tracks for a few seconds and hold his breath. His movements were precise and he made a lot of eye contact with his audience.

At the end, restate the point. You can always rely on a tried and true wrap-up, as in, "The moral of the story is . . . "

Close with something that requires audience participation and a call to action. Leave your listeners with a concrete step they need to take to "make it real." Ask them to jot down a key phrase, or give them a tea bag and tell them to review material over a cup of tea later—anything that makes them take some sort of action.

"A great presentation is kind of like this shish kebab. It's a fast pitch with a hook, a point, some steak, and some sizzle. By presentation I mean anything you do to convince others to take action." He picked up his fork. "The hook get's their attention like a television headline. There's your *A.*" He clicked his fork against the metal hook on the kebab.

"Attention."

"The point tells them why they should be interested. What's in it for them. That's your *I.*" Click. "For interest."

"The steak," he continued, "is the logical stuff—the facts and figures to back up your point so you make sense. The sizzle is the fun stuff, the emotional, memorable, satisfying part to blend together their reason and imagination and tweak their desire. That's *D.*" Another click.

He leaned forward and sniffed the kebab. Then he sat back. "And if the whole thing looks good and smells good, then you roll up your sleeves and . . ." Click, click. "*A* for action. Now let's eat."

I-KOLAs

We munched away in contented silence for a few minutes. Then Muldoon wiped his mouth, took a drink of water, and said, "By the way, that's an 'I-KOLA'"

I nodded. I didn't have a clue what he was talking about but I knew he'd fill me in, so I kept quiet.

"I told you before how a great presentation is like a shish kebab. But a shish kebab is just one of three techniques to get people to act on your ideas. In fact, when I say, 'a great presentation is kind of like a shish kebab,' I'm actually using a second technique. I call that one I-KOLA. I-KOLA is an acronym composed of the initial letters of the words *'is kind of like a.'* Need an example? How about, 'Our new monitoring system is kind of like a palm tree. It lets us . . . ' Or 'Martha deals with traffic jams kind of like a cleaver deals with meat.' It's a way to represent a complicated concept with a simple picture. An image of a shish kebab is a lot easier to remember than several pages of data. Remember, Nicko, facts and figures fade fast, but a picture, or a story, lasts forever."

"Like today," I responded, "when you said, '*Woman* magazine is kind of like Covent Garden Market.' Colorful. Fresh. Alive."

"You have to use your imagination to capture their imaginations."

It occurred to me if I had to I-KOLA Muldoon, I'd cast him as "kind of like a Christmas tree." Bright, sparkling, comforting, and full of surprises.

I-KOLAs in Action

A client of mine directed his staff of IT engineers and salespeople to "evangelize" their new processing system at every opportunity. Trouble was, nobody could put the benefits of the new system into simple terms. Sure, given ten minutes, each of them could describe how the system worked and bombard you with jargon, but nobody—not even the president of the company—could put it into "evangelizable" language. To solve the problem, we applied Muldoon's I-KOLA technique to the system, and by day's end we had agreed on this description of the software: "GX2 (not the real name) is kind of like traveling with your clients in a glass-bottom boat. You both can see what's going on in the system at the same time."

Another client, a large architecture firm, was grappling with a disconnect between the architects and the company administrators. They were having trouble collaborating because many architects viewed the administrators as a nuisance and the administrators, in turn, saw the architects as uncooperative.

I-KOLAs give people a simple, evocative entry point to a complicated concept.

We applied the I-KOLA technique to their dilemma and came up with the following analogy: "ArchiTech (not their real name) is kind of like an art gallery. The administration makes sure the gallery opens on time, runs smoothly, and pays its bills. The architects are the great artists that everyone comes to see."

Not all I-KOLA statements take the form of "It's kind of like . . . " When he was asked to explain the trade deficit, Warren Buffet said, "Our country has been behaving like a rich family with an immense farm. In order to consume 4 percent more than they produce—that's the trade deficit—we have, day by day, been both selling pieces of the farm and increasing the mortgage on what we still own." Brilliant. He explained a complex subject in a way that a ten-year-old could understand.

Coining an I-KOLA makes complicated concepts sound simple, interesting, and memorable. They are terrific for problem-solving, brainstorming, convincing, motivating, teaching, and getting a grip on personalities and relationships. It should take between three and thirty seconds to deliver an I-KOLA.

Let's take a look at this simple device in action. A while back I was asked to give a keynote speech for a company to help launch a new software system. I arranged a telephone briefing to get up to speed. After ten minutes, the meeting planner realized that, apart from letting everyone know a new system was coming in, he didn't really have a theme for the launch.

"All right," I said. "Let's try something. I want you to say the very first thing that comes into your head to complete the phrase I'm about to say. I don't care what it is, but it has to be the very first thing. Ready?"

(continued on page 260)

EXERCISE

Float Like a Butterfly. Sting Like a Bee

In 1964 Muhammad Ali (then Cassius Clay) turned the boxing world on its ear when he called heavyweight champion Sonny Liston a "big ugly bear" and declared that he himself would "float like a butterfly and sting like a bee." His evocative words are good examples of simile and metaphor. A simile is a way of comparing o ne thing to another by using the words *like* or *as*. "Talking to shipping is like talking to a brick wall" and "the receptionist is as cool as a cucumber" are both similes. A metaphor is almost the same thing, except it doesn't use *like* or *as* to make the comparison. "We are a mighty river carving our own path" is a metaphor, as is "If you can't stand the heat, get out of the kitchen."

For the sake of simplicity, Muldoon lumped similes and metaphors together and called them I-KOLA. Once you get the hang of it, you can omit the "it's kind of like a . . . " if you wish. I-KOLA is just a device to get you going.

Similes

Examples: My checking account is like a bottomless pit. These flight controls are as sloppy as a raw sausage. This air conditioner sounds like someone chopping wood in a submarine.

Your turn:

I make cold calls like a ____________.

My office is as ____________ as a ____________.

Metaphors

Examples: Get out there and blow their socks off. My office is a lion's den. These new interns are swimming upstream.

Your turn:

My boss is a ____________ when he/she's angry.

The hot sun was a ____________ beating down on my face.

Sentence Metaphors

Examples:

Step 1. Select a noun (a person, place, or thing). For example, a car.

Step 2. Find a different noun to compare it to. Let's use a chariot in this example.

Step 3. Use both nouns in a sentence: My car is a chariot at my command.

Your turn:

Step 1. Noun: ____________________________

Step 2. Compare it to: _______________________

Step 3. Sentence: _________________________

____

____

____

"Yep."

"The new software system is kind of like a . . . ?"

There was a brief pause at the other end of the line, then, "I don't know where this came from, but the first thing I saw was a train."

"Great," I said. "Tell me about the train."

"It's been heading in the wrong direction for a long time."

"What else?"

"We've managed to stop the train and turn it around. Now we know where the controls are and we've got the train on the right tracks." He was on a roll. "We're ready to get everyone on board and show them where to sit and then get rolling in the right direction."

"Excellent," I said. "How would you feel about using an 'All Aboard' theme at the meeting?"

It was a simple phrase but good enough to get everyone thinking the same way.

At a workshop for financial planners, I asked the participants to write down the first thing that came into their heads to complete the phrase "I am kind of like a . . . " The idea was to show them how easily they could conjure vivid memorable images. I told them to select anything that came to mind—an eagle, a carrot, a Sherman tank—it didn't matter. Usually the very first thing that comes into your head is the best because it comes from the "creative inner child." Once that inner creative force is reawakened, it will be easier to come up with images in the future.

Next, the participants were directed to take two minutes to extend the comparison. They were asked to jot down whatever came to mind. The participants were surprised and pleased with the results.

One woman said, "I have no idea where this came from. I wrote down that I am kind of like a Rubik's Cube." Picking up her notes, she read, "I'm a puzzle to some people but easy to solve when you know how. I'm colorful and have different sides to my personality."

EXERCISE

Personal I-KOLAs

Conjure an image of a thing to best represent the following aspects of your personal life, just as the people in the workshop for financial planners did. This will get you into the habit of incorporating I-KOLAs into your everyday conversations and reveal the creative side that's always lurking below the surface in your mind.

1. I am kind of like a __________ because __________.
2. My best friend is kind of like a __________ because __________.
3. My job/school is kind of like a __________ because __________.

A man spoke next. "I'm kind of like an ocean," he beamed. "I'm strong and deep. I can be wild or calm. I can lift people up and take them places."

Next another woman chimed in. "I'm kind of like a flower," she said. "What kind of flower?" I asked. "Any

An Image Is Worth a Thousand Words

Recently, I met Najeeba in the green room at *The Early Show* in New York. The show was doing a segment on acing job interviews and had recruited viewers who needed help with this skill. In the ten months prior to the show, Najeeba, an unemployed accounts receivable specialist, had sent out three hundred twenty-nine résumés and gone to seventy-four interviews without landing a single job offer. I spoke to her about the way she presented herself and suggested she think about a personal I-KOLA to highlight what she had to offer potential employers. At the seventy-fifth interview, along with all the skills detailed on her extensive résumé, she said, "I'm kind of like a pit bull. I'm watchful, loyal, and protective." She got the job. Maybe it was just luck, but maybe the offer was made because Najeeba lodged an unshakable positive image in the head of the interviewer.

kind," she said. Not a good enough image, I thought. Why not? Because I couldn't visualize her flower in my mind. I could picture the Rubik's Cube and the ocean, but her image wasn't specific enough. For an I-KOLA to work, the other person has to be able to *see* the same picture that the speaker is visualizing. With this woman, she might be picturing a rose and I might see a sunflower.

Story Speak It

Stories are to the human heart what food is to the body. Advertisers polish them, marketers spread them, lawyers bend them, and religions exalt them. We watch them unfold on the screen, read them in books, and when we can't find one handy, we make them up. And no wonder. We are natural-born storytellers; the skill is in our genes. We learn the basics of storytelling as soon as we learn to talk. By the age of five, we tell stories to wangle, cajole, and get what we want. But for most people, storytelling ends there. We still tell stories, but without the structure to make much of an impact on other people.

Who among us doesn't love to be told a good story?

But stories have played a pivotal role in the lives and careers of movers and shakers. What do you think

Winston Churchill and John Lennon have in common? Or Abraham Lincoln and Martin Luther King Jr.? Not to mention Jesus, Buddha, and the Prophet Muhammad? They all told stories to get attention, capture interest, fire desire, and move their listeners to action.

But they never, ever used a story to outright sell. If you've proved your point and delivered it into the hearts and minds of your listeners, the selling takes care of itself.

Let's say you're introducing a new service, one that you think your sales staff will find unorthodox, but you think is visionary and has potential. You could invoke the story of Aristotle to make your pitch: "When Aristotle said the world was round, they said he was off his rocker . . . "

Or you could cite Aristotle to introduce a story about challenging the status quo, breaking barriers, and having vision.

Where would the human race be today if the likes of Christopher Columbus, the Wright brothers, or the astronauts hadn't followed their dreams? Their stories could introduce your message about leadership, teamwork, or courage.

When Mark Burnett, the producer of *The Apprentice,* told his friends that he was going to make a television show about job interviews, they told him he was nuts. But Burnett was certain that telling his story could be a way to address the merits of determination, innovation, and pushing boundaries.

How to Tell a Story: Stepping-Stones

Telling a good story is like picking your way across a fast-flowing stream on stepping-stones. The stream is the problem, and the stones are the path to a solution. Three stones are usually sufficient. You open the presentation on one bank, step onto the different stones on the way across the stream, and close as you step onto the opposite bank.

At the start, standing at the river's edge, you set up the story and state the point. It's here that you introduce the character(s) (the who), the setting or location (the where), and the time (the when). Stepping onto the first stone you explain the problem, dilemma, or predicament. Moving out onto the second stone in the middle of the fast-flowing stream, you describe one or two failed attempts to resolve the problem before leaping onto the third stone and revealing the successful solution. As you step onto the far bank, you deliver your emotional close and restate your point. As you point to the future, you can invite your listeners to imagine themselves in the same situation, and use what they learned from your story to resolve the problem. Prompt your listeners to visualize how to apply what they've heard: "Just imagine . . . ," "Picture yourself in the future when . . . ," "The next time you are faced with . . ."

Many speakers will physically move from stone to stone as they speak. They actually envision the stones on the ground beside or in front of them and step onto the appropriate stone as they reach that part of the story. This method is called "analog marking," and it links the information you are giving to a specific place on stage in the minds of the audience. If the speaker wants to refer back to something on the bank or one of the stones already crossed, he or she will go back and stand on the imaginary spot again, so the audience will be there with the speaker and recall what they heard earlier.

To illustrate my point, here's a story drawn from my own experience. I use it to express one of my core beliefs: "There's no such thing as failure, there is only feedback."

(On the bank) I live on a farm in a very picturesque part of the Canadian countryside. My neighbor raises horses. On weekends, when people travel from the city to enjoy the sights and sounds of the countryside, they stop and feed the horses over the fences and take pictures.

(On the first stone) "They're driving me nuts," my neighbor told me one Saturday morning. "I don't mind people stopping to take pictures, but they've got to stop feeding the horses. They try to give them hot dogs and hamburgers and leftover pizza. Horses are vegetarians, for heaven's sake! They just sniff it and drop it right there. Monday morning I have to pick up all the debris before it attracts flies and rats and dogs."

(On the second stone in the middle of the stream) "So, I put up a DO NOT FEED THE HORSES sign, but the problem got worse."

"I'm not surprised," I said. "Now all the people who never even thought about feeding the horses see your sign and get the idea, 'Oh, let's feed the horses.'"

"I thought it was because the sign was too pushy. So I changed it to read PLEASE DO NOT FEED THE HORSES, but it's gotten even worse."

"Of course! Probably people now drive by and think, 'Oh what a great idea, let's stop and let Granny and the kids feed the horses. This guy's polite—he says "please"—so he won't mind.'"

(Leaping onto the last stone) "Nick," said my neighbor, "you've got to help me! I'm at my wit's end. I give up."

I scribbled a few words on a scrap of paper. "Try putting this on your sign."

I didn't see him again until the end of summer. One evening his truck pulled up in my driveway and my neighbor got out smiling.

"Nick, your sign worked like magic!"

EXERCISE

Crossing the Stream

Pinpointing the structure of a story can be useful in honing your own stories. Fill in the following about the apples and carrots story:

The point: ______________________________

____

The who: ______________________________

____

The where: ______________________________

____

The when: ______________________________

____

The problem: ______________________________

____

First attempt: ______________________________

____

____

Second attempt: ______________________________

____

____

The resolution: ______________________________

____

____

Looking to the future/The moral of the story: __________

____

____

If you drive by today, you can see the sign for yourself. It reads, WE EAT ONLY APPLES AND CARROTS.

(Stepping onto the far bank) The only time you can fail at something is when you stop processing feedback. Know what you want, make a plan, and take action. But solicit feedback to find out how your efforts are going. Be flexible and change what you do until you get what you want.

(Looking to the future) Just imagine how much more success you can have in your life when you let feedback be your guide.

Top Ten Tests for a Story

Your stories should be tight and to the point. There is no room for digressions or distractions. Check your stories against the ten tests below and adjust them to optimize their performance.

1. Does it address the three key questions: "So what?" "Who cares?" and "What's in it for me?"

2. Does it have a point? Remember: No point? No story. What's your point?

3. Is it different (not just another office story)? Make it interesting, unusual, even triumphant.

EXERCISE

Story Time

It's time to tell some stories. Start by figuring out the key point you want to make and the message you want your listeners to come away with. Once you know your point, you can start pondering your hook. Your hook is anything that arouses your audience's interest and makes them want to know what happens next. The best hooks ask a question (overtly or by implication), introduce a character, introduce the dilemma and/or build anticipation for what's to come.

The most moving stories come from personal experience because they are real and you are standing right there telling them. Your audience will have the advantage of reading the hidden codes in your body language as you tell your story.

Find someone you're comfortable with—your spouse or a friend or family member—and tell him or her stories about the following topics:

1. A challenge you overcame at work.
2. A success you had at home.

Be sure to include the point, along with the "who," "where," "when," and the problem in the beginning, lay out the attempts to solve it in the middle, and offer the solution in the ending. Then figure out what you learned from the experience—the moral of your story.

4. Is it emotional? Does it connect with the emotions of your audience?

5. Does it both show and tell? Besides conveying a timeline of events, does your story describe how things look, sound, feel, smell, and taste? For best effect, it should convey at least some sensory information.

6. Is it short and simple?

7. Could a ten-year-old understand it?

8. Is it entertaining?

9. Does it ring true?

10. Have you avoided overly detailed descriptions of people, places, and things? Have you left out the parts that don't directly affect the story?

Great communicators tell stories to make things more interesting and to connect with and motivate their audiences. The human imagination is nothing more than the uniquely human ability to distort information that comes in through our senses. Great orators and communicators rely on their ability to feed the imagination with what it likes best: images, sounds, feelings, smells, and tastes. Storytelling is especially useful in gaining rapport with groups because stories appeal simultaneously to

EXERCISE

Story Speak

Prepare a story relating to your work—something that will inspire your staff or team. Feel free to look for inspiration on the Internet or in your local newspapers to help you get the hang of it. A story about how a local hockey team overcame getting stuck in a snowdrift for sixteen hours with no food, got dug out just in time to play the league champions, and played to a draw without once complaining might work to motivate a team at the office. Use the checklist on page 269 to test your story.

visuals, auditories, and kinesthetics. In addition, stories make learning easier, quicker, and richer because the information arrives prepackaged and requires no conscious processing. As long as you trust the person who is telling you a story, and his or her words make sense, the stories you hear will be welcomed with open arms by your imagination.

90-Second Summary

Parables, fables, and anecdotes are some of the oldest and most powerful communication tools, and they are effective in virtually every setting. Stories fire up the imagination and appeal to the senses. Everyone loves a good story.

Story Speak builds bridges from the rational side of the human mind to the sensory world; it is a way of linking our internal imagination to external reality. Use it in your everyday communication and in your speeches.

Capture the imagination and move an individual or group to action in four steps: Attention, Interest, Desire, and Action. To do this, you can use three distinct techniques: Shish Kebab, I-KOLA, and Stepping-Stones.

Shish Kebab

A shish kebab has a hook, where you grab your audience's attention; a point, which is your main message; steak, your hard data; and sizzle, something fun to create emotional involvement. It is used to make fast, powerful, memorable presentations.

I-KOLA

An I-KOLA (acronym for "is kind of like a") makes complicated concepts sound simple, interesting, and memorable using lively, accessible similes and metaphors.

Stepping-Stones

Stepping-Stones offer a concrete storytelling structure that engages the audience. It involves setting the scene and the challenge, describing attempts to resolve the problem, then revealing the solution.

Story Speak Benefits

You can use your Story Speak skills in myriad ways, including to:

- pitch ideas to employees, customers, colleagues, shareholders, friends, and family
- bring about changes in behavior, habits, and attitudes
- lead and motivate individuals, groups, and populations
- break down barriers and spark transformations
- keep yourself uppermost in people's minds
- share your values
- make emotional connections and communicate on a personal level
- bring your products and services alive
- simplify complex concepts
- spice up presentations of facts and figures

Most important, remember: No point? No presentation.

13

The Show Must Go On

A few years ago, I was the guest on The *Debra Duncan Show* in Houston, Texas. It was a one-hour special titled *America's Biggest Fear,* and it was about public speaking. The producers had previously solicited viewers who had trouble talking to groups, yet whose jobs required them to make presentations on an ongoing basis. I was supposed to come in and teach them how to overcome this fear. Five people were chosen; three of them chickened out at the last minute.

The day before the show, I had the pleasure of meeting one of them, the heroic Teresa. My job was to guide her from panic to poise. Teresa is a sweetheart, a CPR instructor in her mid-thirties whose job requires her to visit organizations and businesses and teach people how to save lives. The only trouble is that she is petrified of talking to groups.

A few hours before we met, the station had taped her making a presentation to a group of strangers in a small boardroom. The tape was painful to watch because Teresa showed every symptom of panic. She made no eye contact, wore a frozen, pained smile, gulped and

Practice, Practice, Practice

The catch-22 of connecting with groups is that the more you do it, the easier it becomes—the problem is that most of us don't have much chance to gain that experience. Sure, naturally outgoing persuaders and controllers are generally more comfortable than the more introspective analysts and dreamers, but there's no substitute for experience.

There are a lot of ways that you can get that experience. When our children were in their early teens, my wife and I made a deal with them. On the first Tuesday of each month, at supper time, we would "visit" a foreign country. Our five children decided which country they wanted to visit each month, and Wendy and I would research the menu and prepare a typical three-course meal from the chosen destination. During dinner each child agreed to give a short, informal presentation about predetermined aspects of the country—climate, tourism, industry, politics, exports.

We all had a month to prepare. I remember

swallowed every few words, and was standing motionless on what was clearly a pair of weak knees. Finally she just stopped talking, a victim of every speaker's worst

answering the phone on one occasion to be told, "This is the Mexican consulate, may I please speak to Sandy?" She was ten at the time and had phoned asking for information. It subsequently arrived in the mail. At first, the kids were shy and nervous, but before long they were learning from one another how to research and how to make their talks enjoyable and informative. Guests would sometimes join us at the table and get in on the fun—we never took the content very seriously. These entertaining adventures continued for more than a year, and we had a wonderful time.

Today, the kids don't think twice when they have to give a talk or a presentation. Do you think this exercise helped them at school and later on in life? You bet. Do you think it's ever too early, or too late, to start learning a skill as valuable as this? No. Find a way to practice your public speaking skills. You can start small—even by just telling folks at dinner about an interesting article you read in the paper or online. Make sure you have a hook, a point, some steak, and some sizzle (see page 252).

nightmare—brainlock. We reviewed the tape together and spent about an hour going over what she was going to talk about. We didn't write out a speech for her; we just came up with some structure for what she wanted to say. But that wasn't the most important part of our discussion.

I spent a significant portion of our meeting introducing Teresa to a few exercises that might help unlock her potential as a speaker.

"How can you do this for a living?" she asked me.

"Simple. I care deeply about my subject. You can't convince if you don't care. I'm passionate about my topic and I'd never let nerves get in the way."

I needed to find a way to make Teresa care passionately about her subject. "You're in the business of saving lives, Teresa. It's your duty to go out and speak to as many people as you can about CPR. It's your gift. You will save lives by appearing on this show tomorrow. A man, a woman, a teenager, maybe dozens of them over the weeks and years to come, all saved because someone heard you speaking passionately about CPR and was moved to do something themselves. You must spread the word."

It's much easier to be convincing if you care about your topic. Figure out what's important to you about your message and speak from the heart.

Teresa changed her focus from looking inward—thinking about herself and her anxiety—to looking out, thinking about others and how what she had to say could help them save lives. She used her imagination to picture the best outcome of her presentation—an audience caught up in what she had to say—and not the worst (herself, stumbling and embarrassed).

We spent an hour or so going over a few exercises, including Shish Kebab on page 252, and Teresa went home determined to practice what I'd shown her and come to grips once and for all with her debilitating phobia.

The next day at 9:00 A.M. Teresa came onstage in front of a studio audience of 250 people and a viewing audience of many tens of thousands more and talked about her problem with getting up in front of any audience. After ten minutes' conversation, the host asked Teresa if she thought her new outlook would make any difference, and Teresa's response was to ask Debra Duncan for her handheld microphone and to walk out into the audience. For the next three minutes or so, she was asking them questions and telling them about CPR as if she owned the place. Everyone was flabbergasted. Debra Duncan, as intelligent and charismatic a person as you could ever wish to meet, had to chase after Teresa and ask for her mike back, jokingly asking, "Hey, whose show is this, anyway?"

Later, when Debra asked Teresa what contributed

most to her transformation, her reply was a surprise to everyone. She said the most important thing she'd picked up was a breathing exercise I'd given her called "moving your nostrils."

Well, it was a surprise to everyone but me. It had been obvious to me, when Teresa and I were chatting the day before, that her imagination was crippling her. She was gripped with fear at the thought of what she imagined might go wrong. In the same way that you can't get a person to smile by saying "Smile," a photographer knows you can't get someone to relax by saying "Relax." You have to make it happen. The fright in her eyes triggered a memory in me and I told Teresa this story.

My youngest daughter, Pippa, has courageously lived with asthma all her life. In the early hours of the morning several years ago, she awoke having serious difficulty breathing, and her inhaler wasn't helping. I scooped her up and into the car and headed for the breathing machine at the hospital, about twenty miles away from the farm where we live.

After about five miles, her breathing was getting worse. She knew not to panic and so did I, but I desperately wanted to do *something* to help. Out of the blue I remembered something I'd taught myself at boarding school—how to "move my nostrils." Back in those days I'd had a problem with smells. Certain unpleasant smells would make me retch uncontrollably, and a British boarding school is no place to reveal a weakness like that.

I tried dozens of tricks to cope with the problem, but none of them worked. Then one day, out of sheer desperation, I imagined that my nostrils were in the middle of my stomach, and magically, the smell seemed to disappear. This morning in the car with Pippa, I gently asked her to close her eyes and imagine the entrance to a huge cavern, as big as she wanted, right in the middle of her forehead. "And now, let all the air in the world come in and out through the cavern, as much as you want." I talked to her soothingly, and within a minute or two my precious child was calm and relaxed. The crisis had passed.

Let's talk about breathing for a moment. Do you remember the last time someone really startled you? A time when someone ran a red light right in front of you and you thought a crash was inevitable? What was your breathing like when everything was over? Fast, short, shallow—right? That's fight-or-flight breathing, and your whole body responds to that cue—your heart races, your adrenaline surges, and you imagine the worst. You've got to change the paradigm and start from the belly—deep, relaxing breaths.

Before she could "move her nostrils," Teresa needed to start breathing deeper. To get her started with belly breathing, I told Teresa, "Place one hand on your chest and the other just below your navel, and practice

EXERCISE

Square Breathing

Here is another simple breathing exercise to chill you out before a presentation: Inhale slowly, counting to four; hold for four; exhale for four; hold for four. Repeat ten times.

Just as with fight-or-flight breathing, your whole body will respond to this slowing down of the system. You will slow down and your body will relax as it gets the message that "everything's okay."

When you feel comfortable, move up to a count of eight all around, then twelve. A few minutes a day for a week should get you there. You'll take this incredible skill with you to your grave. The only thing is that the better you get at square breathing, and the more you do it, the farther away your grave's going to be.

breathing until the hand on your chest doesn't move at all and the hand on your abdomen moves out with every inhale and moves in as you exhale." She found it easy, and before long she was grinning. Belly breathing allows you to take in almost twice as much air as the chest breathing that most people use, so the first time you do it, it's a nice rush.

Now it was time to move Teresa's nostrils. "As you continue to breathe in and out into your abdomen, imagine your nostrils are just below your navel, and breathe in and out through there directly into your belly." She chuckled. "Oh my, it's so easy."

"Do it again, and this time see if you can smell the coffee." There was a carafe of hot, fresh coffee in the room.

"No, only when I switch my nose back on," she said, and we cracked up.

As long as you're concentrating on your breathing, your phobias will recede. This technique has given liberation to dozens of people: a man scared of elevators, a woman afraid of kitchen knives. On this day in Houston, it gave Teresa the confidence she needed to go out and teach CPR to the state of Texas.

Making Your Point

I told Teresa about the stepping-stones metaphor for shaping a narrative and helped her come up with an opening that would capture her audience's attention and get her point across straightaway. She decided to start with a simple question to immediately involve the audience: "How many of you know what CPR stands for?"

I told her that if you want people to put up their hands, put your own hand up first. When someone answers, include your point when you repeat their answer to the rest of the audience. "Yes, cardiopulmonary resuscitation. And if you keel over right now, I can save your life, because

I know how to do it." Her comment was very Muldoon.

We divided and edited Teresa's message into three piles of information and put one pile on each stepping-stone, complete with straight facts and amusing diversions. Once she got past her opening question—"How many of you know what CPR stands for?"—and all the hands went up, Teresa played with the audience for a few moments with questions, and then stepped onto her first stone. She didn't need notes because she could see what was waiting on the next stone for her. She was using her imagination to work for her instead of against her.

Teresa knew what was waiting on the next stone and the one after that, and she could step ahead whenever she felt ready. Instead of paralyzing her, her imagination let her see, hear, feel, smell, and taste what was coming up and enabled her to share her knowledge.

On the far bank was her emotional close—a true story about a college administrator she had taught, who saved her own father's life at a cocktail party.

America's biggest fear is a testament to the fertile imagination. When imagination comes up against willpower, reason, and logic, it always wins. You can be a slave to your imagination or turn it into a powerful and willing servant. Once you have your imagination under control, you can focus on engaging your audience's imagination, which is the key to real connection and communication.

Practice Makes Perfect

When Mario first contacted me he had just turned forty. He ran a successful sports medicine clinic with more than twenty employees just outside Kansas City. He was a single parent of a teenage boy and girl.

"I have to give a speech to a group of three hundred industry people next year and I'm terrified," he told me. "I've made up my mind to step out of my comfort zone and try to be more relaxed when I talk to large groups."

Some people turn to organizations like Toastmasters to practice their presenting skills. Others turn on the video camera and work on their presentations in their bedrooms or basements. Still others pay fortunes to coaches to choreograph their routines. All these approaches have their merits. But I prefer the simple, natural approach, starting small with things that matter to you.

Here's a challenge: Take up a new activity that involves direct contact with new people.

"I used to love to dance, and I really care about helping people," Mario said, "but I've lost my confidence with strangers, and the idea of getting up in front of a crowd panics me."

I challenged him. "Let's start with your anxiety around

strangers. You say you like to dance and want to help people: Then take salsa lessons and find somewhere to volunteer. If you want results and you're determined, prove it!"

Nine days later, Mario e-mailed me. "I looked for a dance studio in my area but most of them are for cheerleaders. But I didn't give up. A local theater is having auditions for the *Rocky Horror Show.* I'm sure they need

Conquering Last-Minute Butterflies and First-Minute Jitters

Move

Fortunately your mind and body are all part of the same system. You can't feel shy with your hands in your back pockets, you can't feel nervous while jumping in the air with your arms and legs spread wide apart. Just before you go on, find a private place (the bathroom will do) and shake out your body.

At-the-Podium Anxiety

Find a friendly face. They're always out there, the "nodders." God bless them, nodding away, agreeing with you and smiling. They usually make up about 5 percent of the audience. Find three or four and keep coming back to them for comfort.

volunteers. I'm nervous and excited about that. And I've joined a softball league."

Imagine my surprise when I opened his next e-mail two weeks later. "I just wanted you to know I auditioned for *Rocky Horror*. It was scary. But I did it, and I was happy that I had the guts to audition. Well, I got a part. I was hoping just to get chorus in the background or even moving scenery or selling tickets. But they offered me the lead."

Square Breathing

Sometimes you might find yourself in a situation where you can't get up and strut about. Try square breathing to calm you down (page 282).

Blanking Out

Have a life raft. Many speakers, especially those who don't use notes, occasionally blank out. It can be for many reasons. In my case it happens when I give more than one talk in a day. I find myself wondering if I've said that already. Sometimes I have, but it was usually at a previous talk, earlier in the day. Always have somewhere to go. In interactive speeches, I ask questions. Ideally, the questions will be related to your topic ("Has anybody experienced . . . ?"), but they can be as simple as, "Does anybody have any questions so far?"

Mario is not what you'd call tall and slim. It took a lot of guts and determination for him to break out and get involved. With his staff and kids cheering him on opening night, he stepped out and took the plunge. The amateur production ran twenty sold-out shows, and Mario got practice, practice, practice performing in front of an audience.

"I was overwhelmed with fear for ten seconds, then that was it," said Mario. "I broke through the barrier and I loved every minute."

"And so?" I asked after the show closed. "How do you feel now about giving your speech next year?"

"Let me at them," Mario beamed. "If anyone had told me six months ago that my life could be exciting and I could stand up in front of a crowd and not be stuck for words, I'd have said they were crazy. But it happened. Inside I know everyone is creative, but most of us never show it for fear of making fools of ourselves. I was shut down. Looking back, I think I could have stayed that way forever."

Mario gave his speech at the industry convention. He stepped up to the podium and slowly looked out at the audience, and made eye contact with a few individuals. Then he grinned. "I work best under pressure," he declared. "And right now I'm boiling over with excitement." He connected with his audience right away and delivered his speech. They felt his passion. Afterward he was approached by three different people who asked if he'd come and deliver his speech to their staff. And he did.

Success doesn't depend solely on how well you do your job; it also depends on how much you care and how well you connect with people and deliver your message. The ability to stand up and present will take your career and your confidence places you have never imagined. Mario and Teresa learned that speaking to a group is not a matter of duty; it's a matter of passion. Not a matter of nerves, but a matter of practice.

You can start today and follow Mario's lead with this two-step plan.

1. Get involved.

Forgo television, video games, and other pastimes until you have a *new* face-to-face commitment that meets at least weekly—more often is fine—outside the house with *new* people in an activity that involves human contact. Take a class, hook up with an amateur theater or improvisation group, volunteer as a tour guide, man an information desk, join Toastmasters or a community service organization—all these are good options.

2. Stay involved

Attend your face-to-face commitment regularly for three months. Mario wanted to turn tail and run but he didn't. He braved it out and made it work. He e-mailed me recently. He's joined a band with three doctors ("Nick, it's good for business"), is auditioning for a part in *Annie,* and enclosed three pictures of himself skydiving!

Show a Bit of Personality

Harry, a well-known orthodontist, is often asked to give speeches about his methods. He is a fairly serious guy, so he always selects his wardrobe to fall on the side of authority, but in order to be perceived as approachable by his audience, Harry always wears his "spectacular spectacles."

Harry has worn glasses since he was twelve years old. Once, when he was to give the after-dinner speech to the orthodontists' association, his glasses slipped beneath the risers supporting their table and they couldn't be retrieved until the event was over. Fortunately for Harry, his wife, Doreen, had a prescription almost identical to his. Unfortunately for Harry (or so he thought at the time), Doreen was debuting her new glasses that night, the ones with the fashionable milky-white frames.

The show had to go on—so Harry stepped up, white glasses and all. He never made reference to the glasses and went on as if everything was perfectly normal. And he was a hit. In fact, he was a bigger hit that night than he'd ever been before. Afterward, he told Doreen it must have been her glasses that brought him luck. Doreen said he looked like a movie star and bought him a pair for Father's Day. She wrapped them up and gave them to him with a card that read, "You looked spectacular."

Serious Harry connects with the room before he (or anyone in the audience) opens his mouth because these spectacular specs add an approachable note to his authoritative look that is clearly winning.

90-Second Summary

The Art of Presentation

Everything you've learned so far comes into play when making a presentation.

- **Establish credibility and authority** with a really useful attitude, eye contact, a smile, personal packaging, and an engaging tone of voice.

- **Get your point across in the first ninety seconds or less.** Audiences have three questions buzzing through their minds: "So what?" "Who cares?" "What's in it for me?" Nothing exasperates an audience more than not knowing what they are doing there. Your point must contain a cause and effect they can relate to.

- **Care about your subject.** Don't try to be an actor on the stage. Tie yourself to a big idea—something meaningful—and your connection with the audience will come from the heart.

- **Control your breathing.** Use a technique like square breathing (breathe in, counting to four; hold for four; out for four; hold for four—repeat ten times) to help you relax and overcome the fear of public speaking.

- **Show some personality.** Let your personality shine through in your presentation. It will allow you to better connect and communicate with your audience.

- **Include I-KOLAs, Shish Kebabs, and Story Speak.** They direct your audience to their senses—to pictures, sounds, feelings, smells, and tastes, to the realm of the imagination. Use them. They make for a much richer presentation.

"Opportunities multiply as they are seized."

—SUN TZU

Afterword: Where Do We Go from Here?

You now have a host of tools for making connections with and getting your ideas across to clients, peers, and prospects, but there's one last piece of hard-won knowledge that I'd like to pass along. Treat each connection you make as if it's the most important one you've ever made. Because it may be. I say this because I know it's true.

Several years ago, my then fourteen-year-old daughter, Kate, told me that a new aromatherapy store had opened in our local village, about ten miles away from the farm where we live. She asked me if I would take her to see it.

While Kate was exploring the place, I struck up a conversation with the owner, Alexandra. She told me how she had come to open the little store, and then asked what I did for a living. I was just launching my first book at the time.

The next week Alexandra phoned me to say she was having a group of people around to talk about aromatherapy, and would I like to spend twenty minutes talking about my book? I agreed and spent a very pleasant evening connecting with her group of friends. At the end of the evening, three of them asked if I would conduct a training workshop if they put together a group.

They managed to assemble more than forty people and rented a hall in a local hotel. We had a terrific session. One of the young female attendees had brought her cousin to the event. Two weeks later the cousin phoned and asked if I would put on a seminar for seventy members of his networking group. I did. One of the people who attended that session worked for a meeting planning company. He went away and recommended me to his company as a speaker.

My last word: Stay open to opportunity—you never know where your next important connection will be made.

Two years later, I was the opening keynote speaker at the AT&T national sales conference, speaking to a capacity crowd of sixteen hundred people. It was, in their words, "an outstanding success." I haven't looked back since.

Yes, serendipity played a huge role in that string of successes, but just as important was the fact that I was ready to connect when the opportunity came knocking. The moral of the story: Never turn down an invitation from your fourteen-year-old daughter to visit a new aromatherapy store in your village. You never know where your next important connection will be made. The world is full of opportunity if you keep your eyes open for it.